Geography
Revision

Meg Gillett and Jack Gillett

Contents

Page

4–5	Which does what?	Differences between weathering and erosion
6–7	At the cutting edge	Headland erosion – process and features
8–9	Where does it all go?	Transport and deposition Longshore drift and coastal spits
10–11	*Test your knowledge 1*	
12–13	Keeping the sea at bay	Coastal protection measures
14–15	We ALL want to be beside the seaside!	Conflicts of interest (between different groups of visitors)
16–17	Decisions! Decisions!	Resolution of conflict and conservation measures
18–19	*Test your knowledge 2*	
20–21	Granny, how did you used to shop?	Shopping as it was 50 years ago
22–23	Tesco rules – OK?	Modern shopping facilities and trends
24–25	Will there be any shops in the future?	Role of the Internet in future shopping
26–27	*Test your knowledge 3*	
28–29	Head in the clouds?	Rain formation and clouds Hydrological cycle
30–31	Rain, rain, go away…	Types of precipitation Rainfall patterns over Europe
32–33	The forecast for tomorrow is…	Weather forecasting and satellite imagery
34–35	*Test your knowledge 4*	
36–37	Freezing in Finland; sweltering in Spain	Factors affecting the climate over Europe
38–39	Do you ski or swim?	Holidaying in Europe
40–41	Phew…chill out!	Effects of climate on life in Europe

42–43	**Test your knowledge 5**	
44–45	Hello, Brazil!	Images of Brazil
46–47	Reality strikes!	What Brazil is really like
48–49	Splitting the difference	Similarities and differences within Brazil
50–51	**Test your knowledge 6**	
52–53	Brazil versus UK!	Developmental issues and comparison with the UK
54–55	Back to the future!	Brazil's history and change
56–57	Onward and upward?	Trade and the role of MNCs in development
58–59	**Test your knowledge 7**	
60–61	Patterns on the planet	World biomes
62–63	Welcome to our habitat	A tropical rainforest ecosystem: adaptation
64–65	It's a worm's world!	Ecosystem interaction Effects of deforestation
66–67	**Test your knowledge 8**	
68–69	People count	Population distribution and growth
70–71	Well dry!	Resource depletion: water
72–73	Dying for a drink?	Water resource management, conservation and sustainability
74–75	**Test your knowledge 9**	
76–77	Glossary	
78–81	Answers	

Which does what?

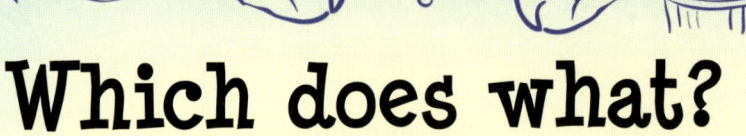

Have you ever looked at a cliff at the seaside and thought: 'Wow! That's impressive! Nothing's ever going to knock that thing down!'? Cliffs are the most stunning things you can see on any coast, and they look strong enough to last for ever. However, most cliffs have thousands of cracks in them. Some of these are very small, while others have expanded into caves big enough to walk into. Cliffs are constantly being worn away, and this can happen in two very different ways: erosion and weathering. These drawings show how both of these processes (natural physical actions) take place.

TYPES OF EROSION

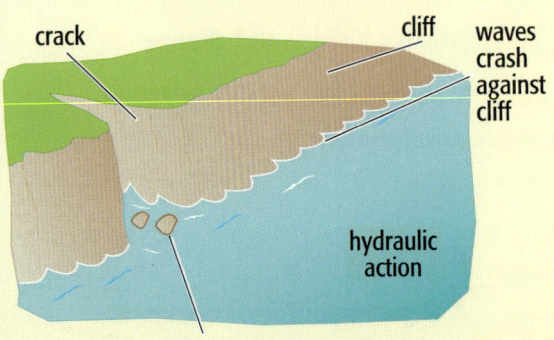

Hydraulic action

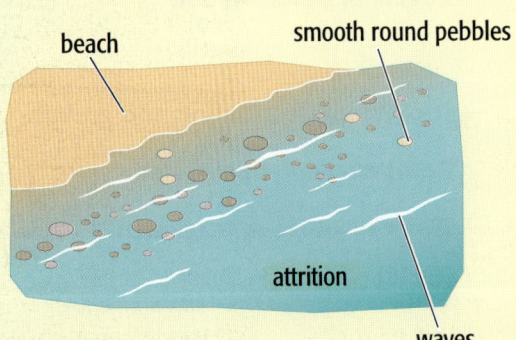

Abrasion

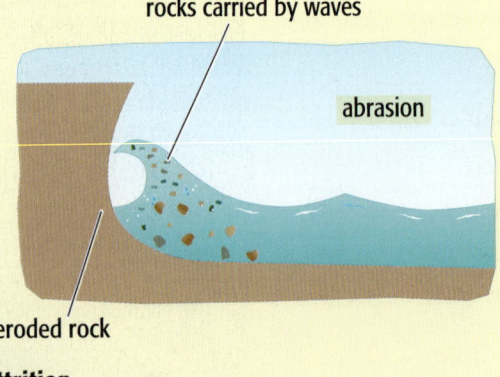

Attrition

TYPES OF WEATHERING

Biological weathering

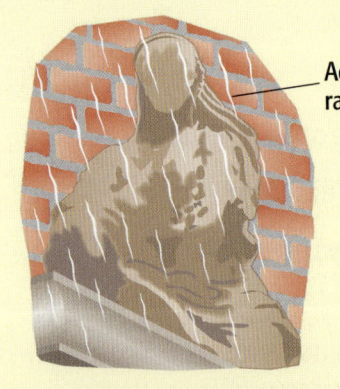

Chemical weathering of stone statue

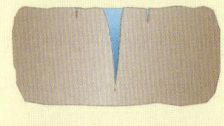
water fills a crack in a rock

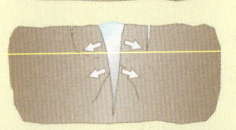
the water freezes and the crack is made wider

the rock breaks into several pieces

Physical (freeze-thaw) weathering

Odd one out

1 Which is the odd one out in this list of key terms?
2 What makes it the odd one out?

   abrasion   attrition   biological action   chemical weathering   cliff   erosion   weathering

Word jumble

Unjumble these words, then write the correct erosion and weathering process in the blanks in these sentences.

   auldrichy ocatin   basionar   chysalip atonic   coolbilagi natico   machlice starconie   notitrait

.... happens when waves smash pebbles onto a cliff.

.... is caused by temperatures changing between hot and cold.

.... happens when pebbles on a beach grind against each other and become smaller, smoother and more rounded.

.... happens when waves trap air inside a crack in a cliff and force the rock apart.

.... is caused by acid rainwater, which dissolves the rock.

.... is caused when growing tree roots force the rock apart.

KEY FACTS

⬆ Many islands in the Pacific Ocean are made of soft coral. Their wave-cut notches can be so wide that they almost cut right through very small islands.

➡ A lot of money has been spent re-laying coastal paths that have been forced up by the biological weathering caused by plants and trees roots. A lot of walkers have had accidents on these uneven paths and sued the local town councils for compensation for the injuries they have suffered from tripping up on them.

⬇ The rocks most easily weathered by chemical weathering are limestone and chalk.

⬆ Every single day, the polluted air in London causes St Paul's Cathedral to lose enough stone to fill ten buckets.

⬅ Physical weathering is most active in rocks that have many cracks in them, such as slate and carboniferous limestone. This is because the cracks give the rock a larger surface area that can be weathered, because it is exposed to the air.

• TOP TIPS •

Remember that weathering happens much more slowly than any erosion caused by the sea and is due to growing plant roots, changing temperatures and the acidic chemicals absorbed by rainwater. Also remember that abrasion erodes rock much faster than the seawater by itself. Try to imagine rubbing your skin with smooth paper, then rough sandpaper – it's the same with rocks.

At the cutting edge

You must have noticed that most coasts are a mixture of bits which stick out into the sea and other bits, in between them, which don't! This happens because headlands (the 'out' bits) are where there are very hard rocks and bays are the spaces where softer rock has been eroded and weathered much more quickly. Most bays are in sheltered places, where deposited sand can form beaches.

As headlands erode, they produce a number of features that are very easy to recognise. These features are usually formed in the same order – starting with quite small cracks in the cliff face. The picture below shows what these features are, and the order in which they are formed. Geos and blow-holes can also help to weaken a headland by splitting it up. Eventually, the end of the headland is completely eroded away, leaving only a gently sloping wave-cut platform where it used to be. These platforms may extend some distance from the shore and be covered at high tide. Such reefs are dangerous places to swim in because of the fast sea currents flowing over them.

Headlands and bays

Erosion crossword

Complete this crossword, which is about headland erosion.

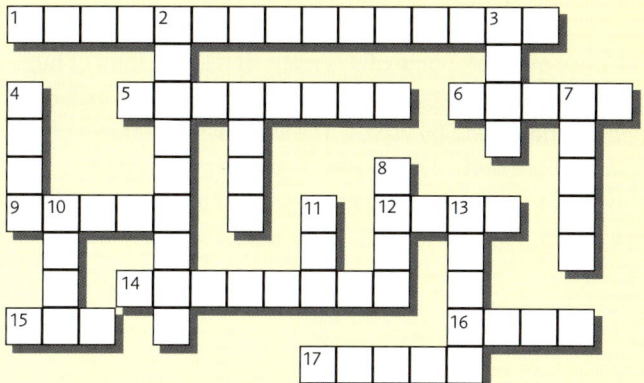

Clues

Across
1. Gently sloping surface of rock exposed at low tide.
5. Formed when a cave roof collapses and water is forced upwards by the rising tide.
6. Area of deposited material along the shoreline.
9. Remnant of 17 Across after more erosion.
12. Opening through a headland.
14. Area of coast that extends out into the sea.
15. 13 Down – much widened by wave action.
16. Hollow formed by waves at the base of a cliff.
17. Pillar of rock surrounded by sea.

Down
2. Falls down?
3. Alternative name for 1 Across.
4. Separate headlands from each other.
7. Steep rock outcrop along the coast.
8. Material found at 6 Across.
10. Twice daily rise and fall of the sea.
11. Salt water but not an ocean.
13. Opening of a line of weakness in a cliff face.

• TOP TIPS •

Erosion isn't the only reason for the disappearance of some of our coast. The world's air temperature is rising, which means that a lot of the solid ice in Antarctica and around the North Pole is melting. Extra water pours into the oceans, causing sea levels to rise and coastal areas to become flooded.

KEY FACTS

↑ The coast around Swanage is broken up by lots of headland and bays. The map shows how its different rocks have helped to shape this part of the Dorset coastline.

→ Marsden Rock is a famous landmark on the Yorkshire coast. It was once a massive 30 m high limestone arch. In 1996, the top part of the arch collapsed – leaving two separate stacks. This rockfall made the smaller stack so unstable and unsafe that its owners had it blown up with explosives!

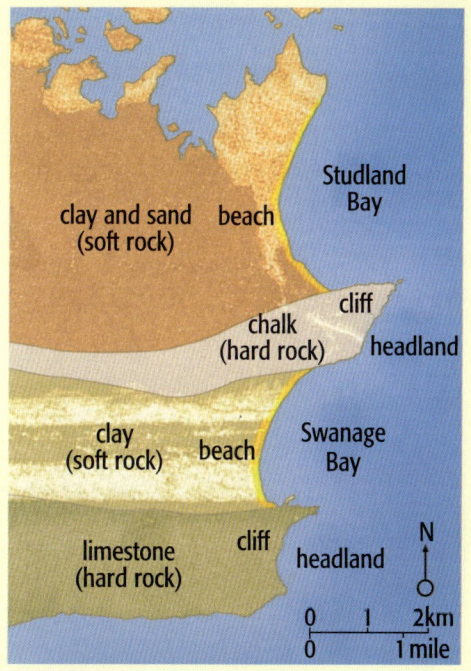

Coastline around Swanage

Where does it all go?

The erosion of headlands produces large amounts of loose material. Some of this material is in the form of huge boulders, which can only be transported (moved) by the sea during violent storms. Most of it is loose material such as sand and pebbles, which can easily be picked up and carried by waves. The sideways movement of material along a beach is called longshore drift (*not along*shore drift). This process is due to swash and backwash – the upward and downward movement of waves on a beach. You can easily test this for yourself by throwing a piece of wood into the sea, then watching how it is moved up, down and along the beach by the wind and the waves.

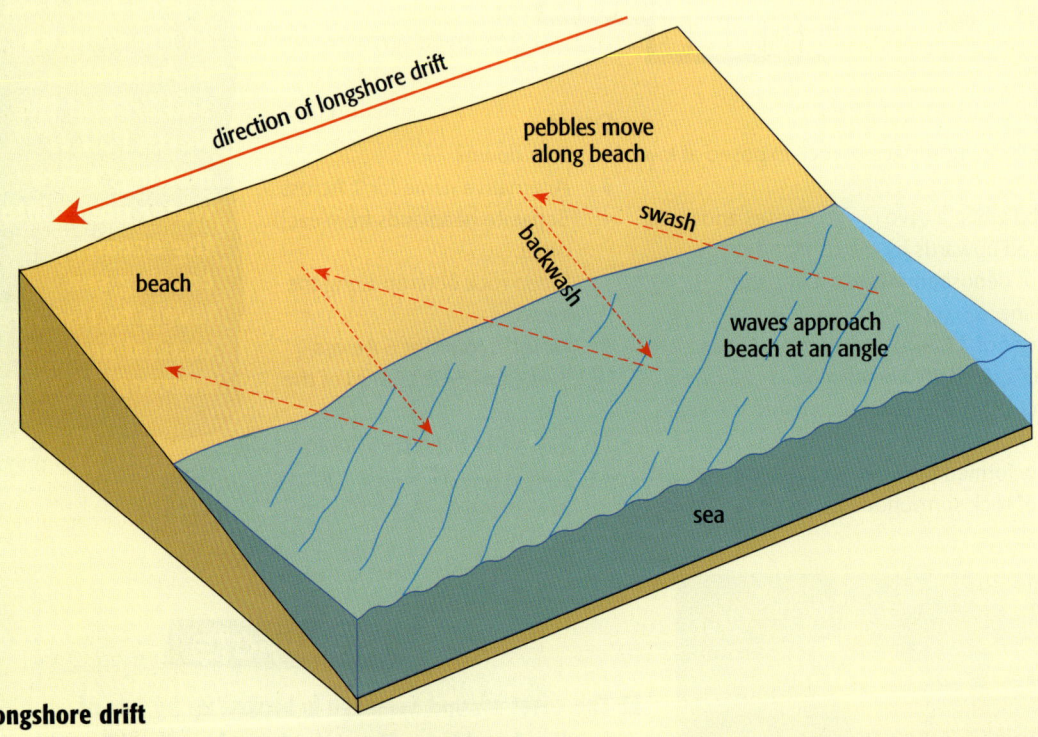

Longshore drift

All the material that moves along a coast has to end up somewhere. Some sinks to the bottom and makes the sea shallower. A lot of it is transported much further along the coast until it comes to a more sheltered place where it is deposited (dropped). The map opposite shows how deposited material can build up, forming new ridges of sand and pebbles called spits.

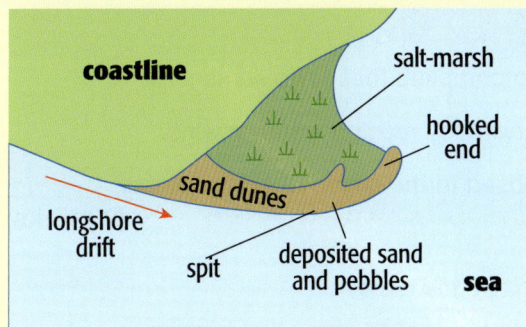

· TOP TIPS ·

When the cliffs on a headland are eroded, the sand and pebbles formed from its rock are transported along the coast by longshore drift. Some of this material is deposited further along the coast, where it forms long, curved ridges called <u>spits</u> in the more sheltered places.

Name the features

Complete this cross-section drawing of a typical spit by writing these terms in the correct label boxes.

sheltered lagoon   mainland   new saltmarsh   sea and longshore drift   spit made of sand or pebbles

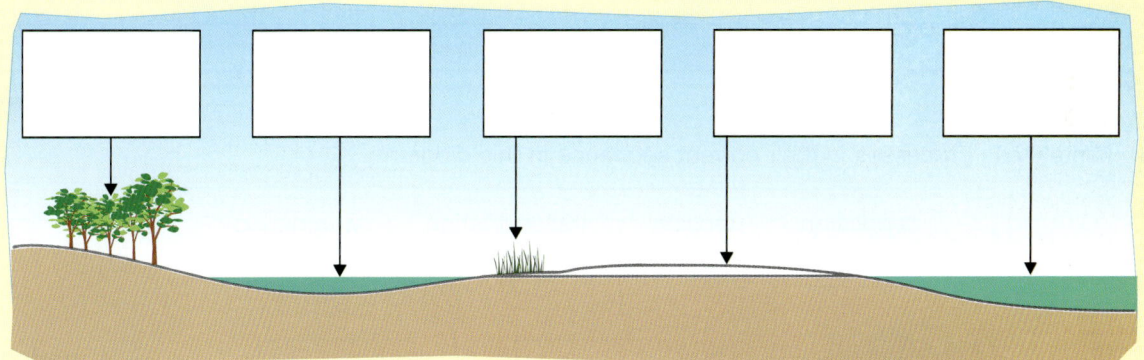

Spit formation

KEY FACTS

⬆ **Hurst Castle Spit, on the south coast of England, is so big and solid that King Henry VIII built a castle on its end to protect us against invasions from across the English Channel.**

➡ **Some of the spits on the east coast of England point southwards, while others point westwards. This map shows the directions of all the main spits on the coasts of England and Wales, and the reasons why they point in these directions.**

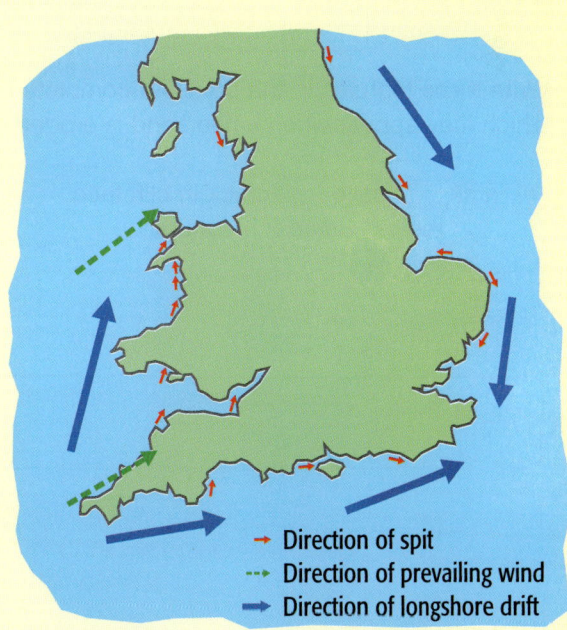

Spit directions around the coast of Britain

Test your knowledge 1

1 Write *erosion* and *weathering* in the blank spaces to complete these two sentences.

.... happens when rock is worn away by moving water or wind.

.... happens when a rock is exposed to the action of acidic rainfall, changing temperatures and growing plants.

(2 marks)

2 Put these six processes under their correct headings in this table:

> abrasion   attrition   biological action   chemical reactions
> hydraulic action   physical action

Erosion processes	Weathering processes

(6 marks)

3 Write these processes in their correct sequence in this diagram:

> deposition   erosion   transportation   weathering

(4 marks)

4 Write these features in the boxes to complete this flow diagram and show the correct order in which they appear when a headland is eroded over many years:

> arch   cave   crack in cliff face
> reef   stack   stump

This appears first

This appears last

(6 marks)

5   Use the *same six labels* to name the features in this drawing of a typical headland that is being eroded by the sea.

(6 marks)

6   Use these labels to complete this map of a coastline that has areas of hard and soft rocks and is being eroded by the sea:

softer rock
very hard rock
headland
erosion is faster here
erosion is very slow here
sheltered bay

(3 marks)

7   What kind of natural feature is shown in this photograph? ....

Aerial photograph of Spurn Head, Humberside

(1 mark)

8   Is *erosion* or *deposition* the main reason for this feature being here? ....
(1 mark)

9   What are the curved parts at the end of this feature called? ....

10 Why does salt marsh often develop between a spit and the lagoon behind it?

....

....

(3 marks)
(Total 32 marks)

Keeping the sea at bay

Visitors want wide sandy beaches, but some of the best beaches are disappearing. This is because headlands erode away *much* more slowly than longshore drift can remove the material from the beaches. So, what happens? Beaches lose far more sand than they receive, which is a real worry for holiday resorts. These pictures show two ways in which resorts can tackle the problem:

- building groynes
- starting beach replenishment.

There is an even bigger worry for towns built on cliffs made of soft rock. At high tide, or during storms, the sea can quickly erode the base of these cliffs, undercutting them and making their tops overhang. It doesn't take long for the obvious to happen! But building sea walls and putting gabions and rock armour in front of the cliffs can greatly reduce the damage done to them by the sea.

Groyne on a beach

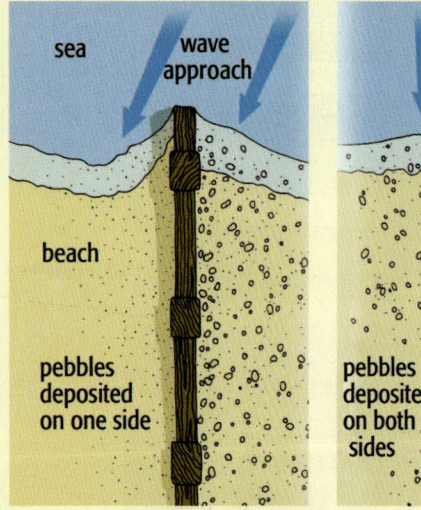

A series of groynes along a beach

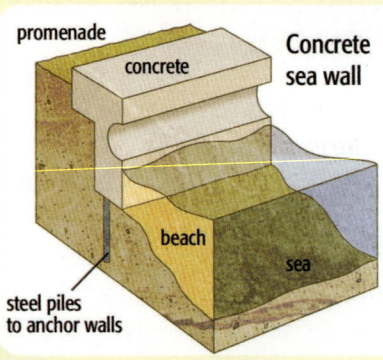
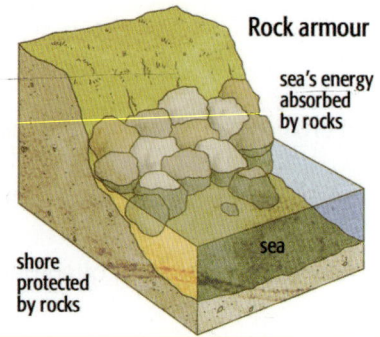

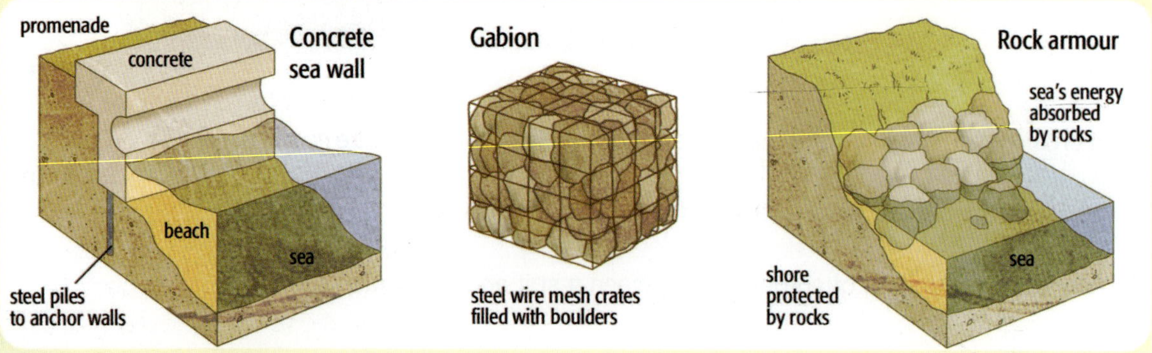

Beach protection measures

Coastal protection

This Venn Diagram has three overlapping circles. Each of its circles shows different kinds of material used in coastal protection methods. Complete the diagram by writing each of these protection methods inside its correct circle or overlapping area:

> beach replenishment   gabions   groynes   rock armour

'Sea walls' has already been added to show you how to do this.

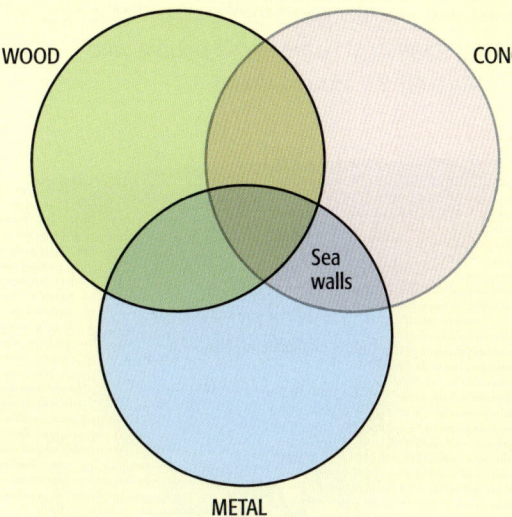

• TOP TIPS •

Sea walls are effective and last a long time, but they cost a lot of money. Replenishing beaches with sand is much cheaper, but it has to be repeated every year because of longshore drift.

KEY FACTS

⬆ Holderness is a 50 km-long stretch of coast, lying between the headland of Flamborough Head and a 6 km curved spit at its southern end called Spurn Head. The cliffs of Holderness are made of very soft clay, which is why it is one of the world's most rapidly eroding coasts. These cliffs erode inland on average two metres every year, which is 200 times faster than the hard limestone of Flamborough Head. These cliffs have retreated so far that 30 villages have already been swept away by the North Sea since the Roman invasion 2000 years ago. Hornsea and Mappleton are two of its villages that still survive, because they have been protected by concrete sea walls, wooden groynes and granite rock armour.

Holderness Coast

We ALL want to be beside the seaside!

People love visiting Britain's beaches – especially on sunny days, when the sea isn't too cold and there isn't a gale force wind! This is because there are so many different leisure activities to do on beaches. Beaches can also be healthy places to visit. The air is clean and fresh, the sun makes you feel happy, there is space for playing games and families can enjoy doing things together. Seafood is really good for you too – as long as it isn't covered in batter and eaten with piles of chips! This drawing shows just some of the people who visit beaches to enjoy themselves, although sometimes they may disturb others around them!

Seaside wordsearch

This wordsearch has 20 beach activities. Ring all its activity words, which can be found along straight lines in *any* direction on the wordsearch.

B	I	R	D	W	A	T	C	H	I	N	G	E	W	S
A	U	R	E	L	L	A	B	Y	E	L	L	O	V	D
S	G	I	C	A	L	O	W	B	R	Y	O	T	I	R
D	F	T	L	E	I	L	S	U	N	B	A	T	H	E
F	D	E	I	D	A	H	G	R	E	L	A	X	D	A
G	S	A	M	I	S	R	K	Y	W	E	L	O	E	D
H	A	S	B	O	P	A	D	D	L	E	L	K	I	M
Q	U	D	C	U	E	R	N	A	U	R	R	S	I	K
W	M	I	L	R	S	G	O	D	K	L	A	W	R	E
E	N	F	I	S	H	O	L	W	C	A	S	W	A	E
R	B	O	F	E	L	J	T	E	Y	A	L	P	A	P
T	E	O	F	R	I	L	L	O	R	T	S	A	D	F
Y	D	M	S	U	R	F	E	R	I	A	E	T	I	I
G	N	I	I	K	S	R	E	T	A	W	E	M	L	T
C	R	B	W	W	D	O	N	K	E	Y	R	I	D	E

Beach pairs

Pair up any six beach activities that could lead to <u>conflict</u> between people wishing to do different things, then suggest a reason for each pairing. The example shows how to do this.

First activity	Second activity	Reason for conflict between people doing these two activities at the same time near to each other
Reading	Playing football	Football is a noisy game, which will disturb people who want to be quiet so they can read a book.

KEY FACTS

- No one in Britain lives more than 112 km from the coast.
- Britons living inland make well over 350 million pleasure visits to the seaside every year.
- Scarborough was Britain's first coastal holiday resort. 250 000 people now live in and around Blackpool and more than 500 000 people live in the Brighton area.
- Beaches that pass quality inspections are allowed to fly the European Blue Flag and the Seaside Award Flag. These flags tell visitors that a beach is safe to use, that it has good toilets and other facilities and that its seawater is not polluted.

• TOP TIPS •

People want to visit the coast, or even live by it, for lots of reasons. The most popular beaches can become very overcrowded at peak holiday times, and this can lead to environmental problems such as litter, noise and polluted seawater.

Decisions! Decisions!

Coasts are places where many people work. Some have jobs in tourism. Others are involved in <u>economic activities</u> that can cause conflicts which are much more serious than those that take place on a pleasure beach!

A lot has been done recently to protect our most attractive and overcrowded stretches of coast:

- Organisations like the National Trust have bought land, because this gives them total control over what can be done with the land they own.
- The government has also helped, by including some of the best coasts in our <u>National Parks</u>. Most of the land in these parks is privately owned, but there are strict planning regulations to prevent any new developments that might ruin their landscapes.
- Much smaller, but still very precious areas include <u>nature reserves</u>, where rare plants and animals can be protected.

Word jigsaw

Complete this 'word jigsaw' by writing the groups of letters in the correct places on the puzzle. It is best to do this in pencil and have a rubber handy!

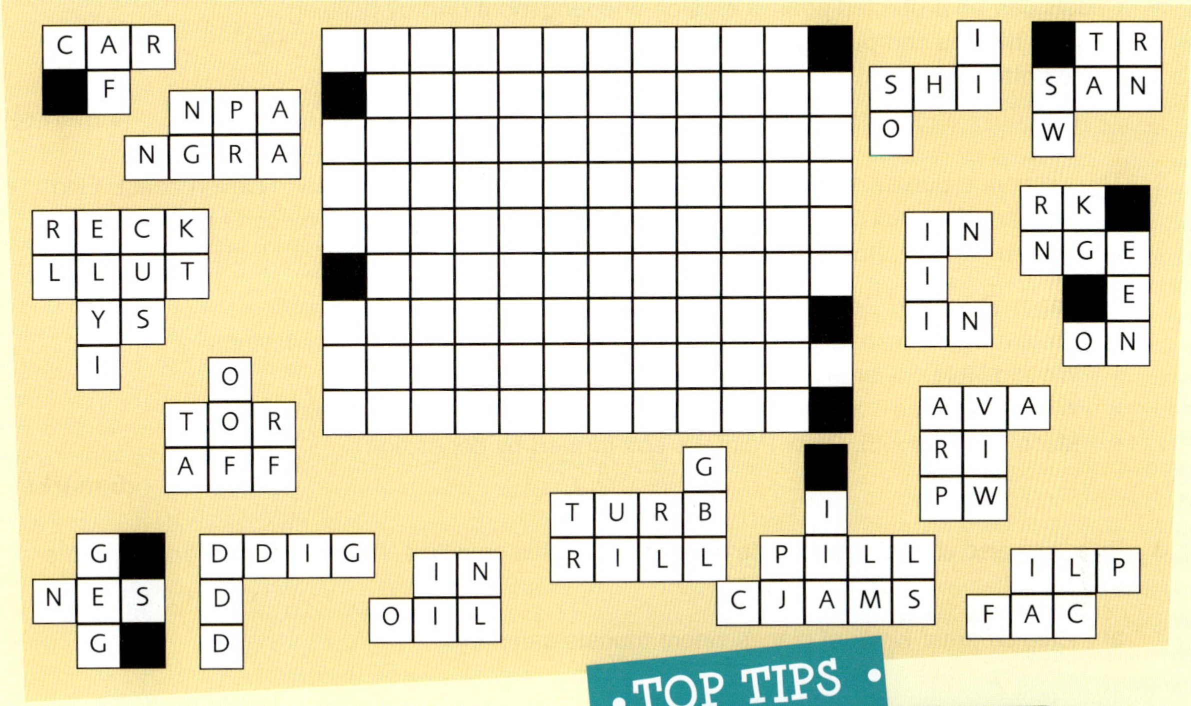

TOP TIPS

Britain has about 55 million people, which is a lot of people for an island only 1000 km from corner to corner (Land's End to John o'Groats). Much of our coast has already been used to build ports, industrial cities and holiday resorts. Even more pressure is being put on our coasts by the growing number of older people who want to live by the seaside when they retire.

KEY FACTS

- ⬆ Britain's coastline is about 10 000 km long and the National Trust owns one-tenth of it.
- ➡ Britain has 14 National Parks and six of these are on the coast.
- ➡ South Downs is a newly designated National Park.
- ⬇ The Pembrokeshire Coast National Park is unique, because it is our only National Park to have been created just to protect the coastline.

Britain's National Parks

Test your knowledge 2

1 Fill in the blank spaces below:

Coasts can be protected against erosion and longshore drift by building .... down to the sea and putting ...., ... and ....
at the bottom of cliffs.

(4 marks)

2 The Ordnance Survey map on the opposite page shows part of the North Devon coast. Find these named features on the map, then turn back to earlier pages if you can't remember how weathering, erosion, transportation and deposition have helped to produce them.

- Baggy Point and Downend Point – headlands made of very hard rock.
- Croyde Bay – in an area of much softer rock between these two headlands.
- Whiting Hole – a large cave on the northern tip of Baggy Point.
- Wheeler's Stone – an island reef that used to be part of Baggy Point.
- Much further south, Crow Point – a spit formed by deposition.

(5 marks)

3 This map also shows how people have changed this coastline. Use information *only from the map* to list:

a) three *different* kinds of places where tourists can stay

b) three *different* kinds of tourist attractions and facilities apart from accomodation

c) three kinds of jobs that local people can do – *not* including jobs in tourism!

d) two ways in which the wildlife and the natural physical features along this coast have been protected by organisations

(11 marks)

(6 marks)
(Total 27 marks)

Granny, how did you used to shop?

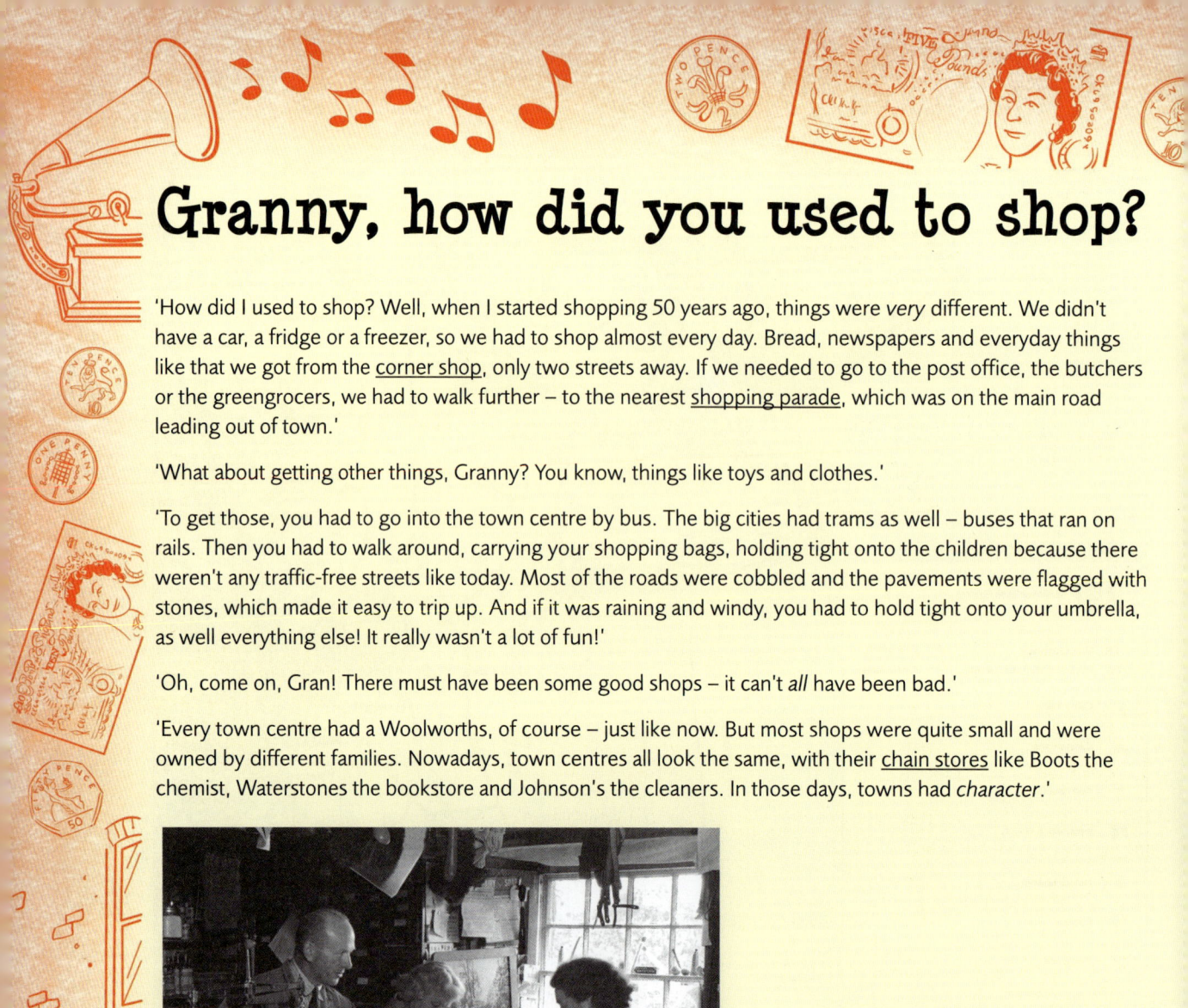

'How did I used to shop? Well, when I started shopping 50 years ago, things were *very* different. We didn't have a car, a fridge or a freezer, so we had to shop almost every day. Bread, newspapers and everyday things like that we got from the corner shop, only two streets away. If we needed to go to the post office, the butchers or the greengrocers, we had to walk further – to the nearest shopping parade, which was on the main road leading out of town.'

'What about getting other things, Granny? You know, things like toys and clothes.'

'To get those, you had to go into the town centre by bus. The big cities had trams as well – buses that ran on rails. Then you had to walk around, carrying your shopping bags, holding tight onto the children because there weren't any traffic-free streets like today. Most of the roads were cobbled and the pavements were flagged with stones, which made it easy to trip up. And if it was raining and windy, you had to hold tight onto your umbrella, as well everything else! It really wasn't a lot of fun!'

'Oh, come on, Gran! There must have been some good shops – it can't *all* have been bad.'

'Every town centre had a Woolworths, of course – just like now. But most shops were quite small and were owned by different families. Nowadays, town centres all look the same, with their chain stores like Boots the chemist, Waterstones the bookstore and Johnson's the cleaners. In those days, towns had *character*.'

Shopping list

Unjumble these things to buy, then put them into the correct column in this table:

funmiro shlooc   grusa   nits fo rdenco febe   snapwereps   soyt
swelto   trubet   funturie

Things you could buy at the corner shop	Things you could only buy in the town centre

• TOP TIPS •

Things that are needed almost every day and are cheap to buy are called <u>low-order goods</u>. More expensive goods like furniture are <u>high-order goods</u>. High-order goods used to be bought in the town centre – the <u>central business district</u> (<u>CBD</u>, for short).

Days gone by

Here are some things that people bought 50 years ago, but which aren't used any more. Try to work out which of these words starts each sentence! *Gramophone; mangle; scrubbing board; wireless.*

A .... is the old word for a radio.

A .... was used to get the dirt out of washing.

A .... was used to play records.

A .... was used to squeeze the water out of washing.

KEY FACTS

⬆ **The corner shop would take a family's weekly order for groceries and other essentials – and their money at the same time. It would pack the order in a box and leave it on the doorstep, which was not always a good idea because it could get rained on or stolen before people came home from work.**

➡ **Most shops had a Christmas Club. Credit cards hadn't been invented, so most people paid a small sum into their clubs each week to save up for presents and extra food at Christmas.**

⬇ **The Co-operative Society (or Co-op) stores were very popular 50 years ago. They gave dividend stamps, which could be exchanged later on to buy other things. The more you spent, the more stamps you received. You could even get stamps from having a Co-op funeral.**

Tesco rules - OK?

If you are one of the 32 000 people who live in Bicester (pronounced 'Bister' by the locals), Tesco is the shop for you. This town in southern England already has *six* Tesco stores, and a seventh one is being planned: that is one Tesco store for fewer than 5000 people.

What is it that makes Tesco so big – and so popular? Like all businesses, Tesco started in a very small way – with a man called Jack Cohen. He had a stall on an open-air market in London's East End and his motto was 'Pile 'em high and flog 'em cheap'. People knew they would always get a bargain at Jack's and he opened his first high street shop in 1932. His Tesco company began later. Three other mottos that helped Jack's new company to grow were: 'Be everywhere! Sell to everyone! Sell everything!' Tesco did this and is now Britain's biggest company in the retail (shopping) trade. The photographs show three kinds of Tesco shop.

A small Metro store in a town centre

A large Tesco supermarket on a retail park on the edge of a town

A huge Tesco hypermarket in a regional shopping centre

What has happened to the corner shops that were so popular 50 years ago? Most have closed down, or have been converted into houses or demolished when the older parts of our towns were rebuilt. Those still trading have joined chain store groups like Londis, Nisa and Spar – to help keep their prices down and compete with big stores. Many people now do their local shopping when they top up the petrol in their car at a garage. Of course, Tesco and the other supermarket giants like Sainsbury and Morrison have their own garages and forecourt shops.

Where do you shop?

The different kinds of shopping places in are shown in this shopping hierarchy. Use all the information on this double page to write these three missing labels onto the diagram. At the bottom of the order should be shops selling convenience goods. At the top are the shops selling high order goods (e.g. furniture, electrical goods.)

- High street shops
- Newsagents, corner shops and petrol station shops
- Retail park with warehouse stores

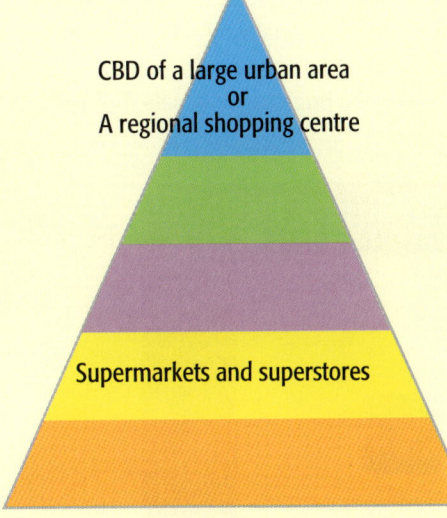

Major out-of-town shopping centres

KEY FACTS

↑ The first supermarkets were built in the 1970s. They sold a wide range of non-food items as well as groceries – some of them having the company's own brand name. These shops proved so successful that even bigger stores, called hypermarkets, were built later on.

→ In the 1980s, large out-of-town retail parks were built. They had DIY (do it yourself), carpet and furniture stores in big, warehouse-type buildings.

↓ The first regional shopping centres were built in the 1990s, on huge sites near to motorways and major cities. The map shows where they are and how many shops each one has. All these centres have car parks for thousands of cars, their own bus services and a wide range of attractions such as cafés and multi-screen cinemas.

TOP TIPS

Increased car, fridge and freezer ownership has completely changed shopping habits over the last 50 years. Families can now drive to a wide range of retail sites, do a whole week's shopping in one visit and even have a meal and enjoy themselves while they are there. For those people who want to avoid road traffic, there are new pedestrianised streets and indoor shopping malls in most town centres.

Will there be any shops in the future?

Would you want to buy *everything* you needed over the Internet? Probably not, because the Internet wouldn't be much help if you suddenly felt like eating a bag of sweets or crisps. But more people *are* using it each year to do most of their shopping.

It has been possible to buy goods without actually going shopping for many years. For example, busy working people, disabled people and people living a long way from the nearest town have been able to order goods from mail order catalogues.

Most companies now have websites to give customers information about their goods and services and some use the Internet for all their trade. Amazon was one of the first to do this —originally by selling books, but now offering DVDs, games and toys as well. eBay is one of the fastest-growing Internet trading companies and is used by people wanting to sell goods they no longer need. It is a bit like a huge car boot sale, but without the traffic congestion, crowds of people and bad weather!

Regional shopping centres like the Trafford Centre in Manchester have their own Express Checkout Internet sites, which allow people to compare prices in all its stores before placing and paying for just one order. This display shows the ten categories of goods included in this one-stop shopping scheme.

Internet – good or bad?

Write 'A' in the box by the following *advantages* (the good things) of shopping on the Internet and 'D' by the disadvantages.

☐ Companies that only trade on the Internet don't need expensive high street shops.

☐ Disabled people can shop without having to leave their home.

☐ Internet shopping stops shoplifters stealing goods and this keeps prices lower.

☐ People won't be able to test drive a car before choosing the model they want.

☐ You can buy goods that are only sold in other countries.

☐ You can order presents and have them posted direct to your family and friends.

☐ You can't see whether clothes fit properly before you buy them.

☐ You can't suddenly buy basic things like bread and milk when you run out of them.

☐ You might be out at work or on holiday when big items are delivered.

Follow the order

Complete this Internet shopping flow diagram by writing these stages in the order you think they happen:

> Chosen items taken off the shelves and packed
> Goods sent by post
> Internet server sends your order to the company's warehouse
> Log on to your chosen company's website
> Parcel arrives at your home
> Place your order on the webpage

KEY FACTS

↑ **The most remote island in the world is Tristan da Cunha, which is in the middle of the South Atlantic Ocean and 2800 km from the nearest land. Its 276 people can now shop on the Internet, because they have just been given their own post code – TDCU 122.**

→ **Nearly 10% of all the books bought in the UK are ordered from Amazon over the Internet.**

↓ **400 000 people in the United States now earn a living by trading with eBay.**

TOP TIPS

The new supermarkets, hypermarkets and regional shopping centres have forced many town centre shops to close. They have reduced traffic congestion, noise and air pollution in the centres, but made them much worse in other areas. Internet shopping could help to make the lives of people in these newly-affected areas safer, healthier and more enjoyable.

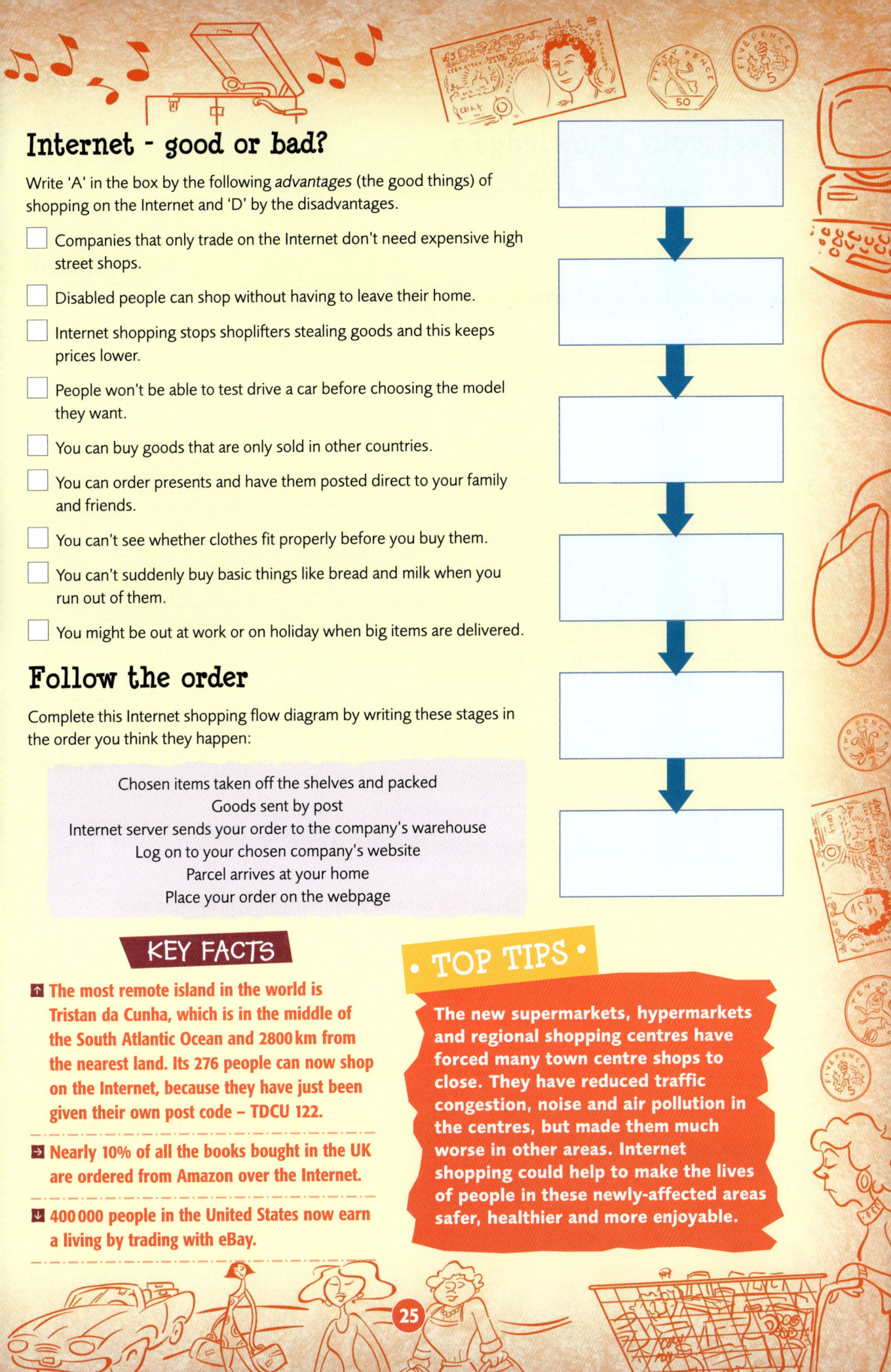

Test your knowledge 3

1 Name the trade that has to do with the buying and selling of things.

....

(1 mark)

2 Finish this table by writing these types of goods in their correct columns:

> black and white TV   bread   comics and magazines   furniture   milk
> potatoes   shoes   sweets   washing machine   watches

Low-order goods	Higher-order goods

(10 marks)

3 What two kinds of shop have replaced many old corner shops?

....

....

(2 marks)

4 Which is bigger: a *supermarket* or a *hypermarket*? ....

(1 mark)

5 List five different things you might *do* in a regional shopping centre, apart from shop.

....

....

....

....

(5 marks)

6 a) Write these regional shopping centre names in their correct boxes on this map:

Bluewater   Braehead   Cribb's Causeway   Lakeside
Meadowhall   Merry Hill   MetroCentre   Trafford Centre

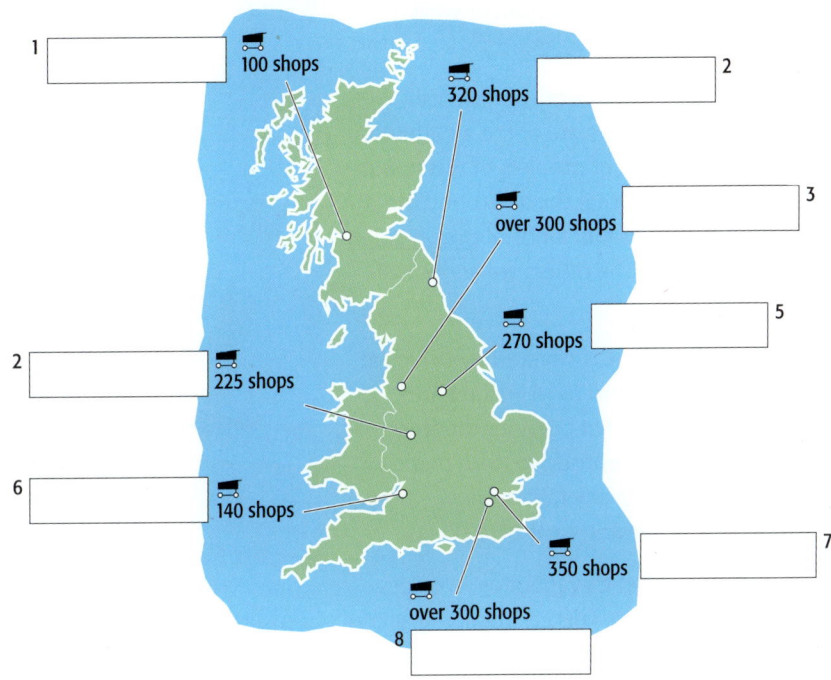

b) Which British city has *two* of these centres? ....

c) Which of these regional shopping centres is in Scotland? ....

d) Does Wales have any of these centres? ....

(11 marks)

7 Cars are one invention that has changed our shopping habits over the last 50 years. List another four inventions that have done the same.

....

....

(4 marks)
(Total 34 marks)

Head in the clouds?

Everyone has daydreamed and looked for cloud pictures or patterns in the sky. Have you ever wondered what clouds are made of, where they come from or what happens to them?

Clouds are one of the main features of what we call weather, which is the day-to-day state of the air around us. Clouds are usually made up of droplets of water, but these become tiny particles of ice if the air around them is very cold. Rain is only one of four kinds of precipitation that are produced by clouds. The others are snow, hail and sleet.

About 60% of the Earth's surface is covered by clouds at any one time. Clouds are essential to all life on Earth, because they produce the rain that provides the fresh water it needs. You might be surprised to learn that over 90% of all clouds *don't* produce any rain or snow – they simply dissolve into the air, leaving clear blue skies.

When water is heated, some of it evaporates (changes from a liquid into water vapour). This is happening all the time over rivers, lakes and seas – and it happens even faster in our homes when kettles and cooking pans are heating up. Warm air can hold more water vapour than cold air so, whenever air becomes cooler, some of its water vapour condenses into liquid droplets. Warm air rises because it is lighter than cold air, but it cools on its way up. Some of its water vapour condenses into droplets, clouds form and rain falls.

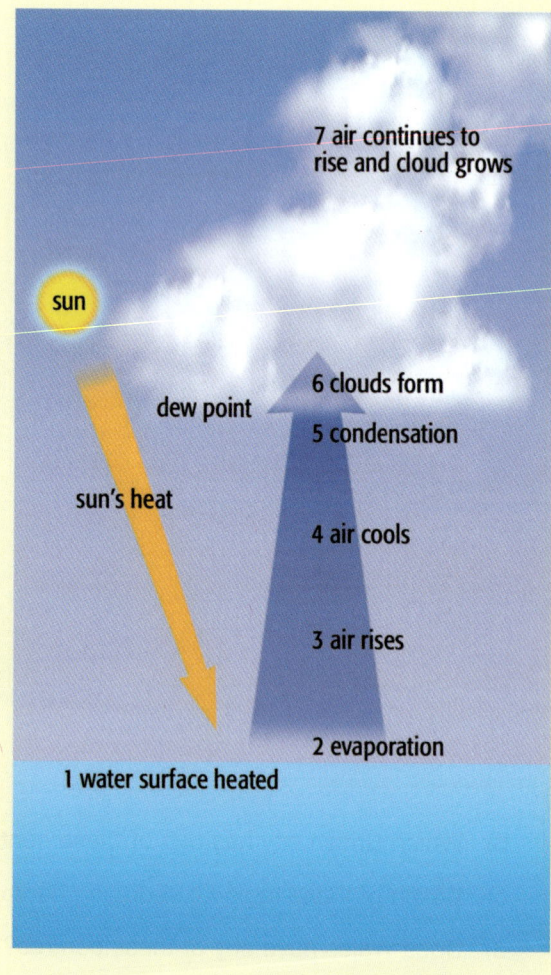

7 air continues to rise and cloud grows

sun

dew point

6 clouds form

5 condensation

sun's heat

4 air cools

3 air rises

2 evaporation

1 water surface heated

There are many different types of cloud, but three main cloud groups. These photographs show how the shape, thickness and height of a cloud all determine which group it belongs to.

Rain cannot fall unless there are clouds in the sky, which makes them a very important part of the hydrological (or water) cycle.

Cumulus

Stratus

Cirrus

Rain jumble

Unjumble these words to find the four different types of precipitation:

Estel is .... *Nari* is ....

Ilah is .... *Nows* is ....

Raindrop routes

Rain falls on surfaces, such as roof tiles and tarmac roads, as well as on natural surfaces. Follow the routes of the two rain drops in this sketch and find out where they end up!

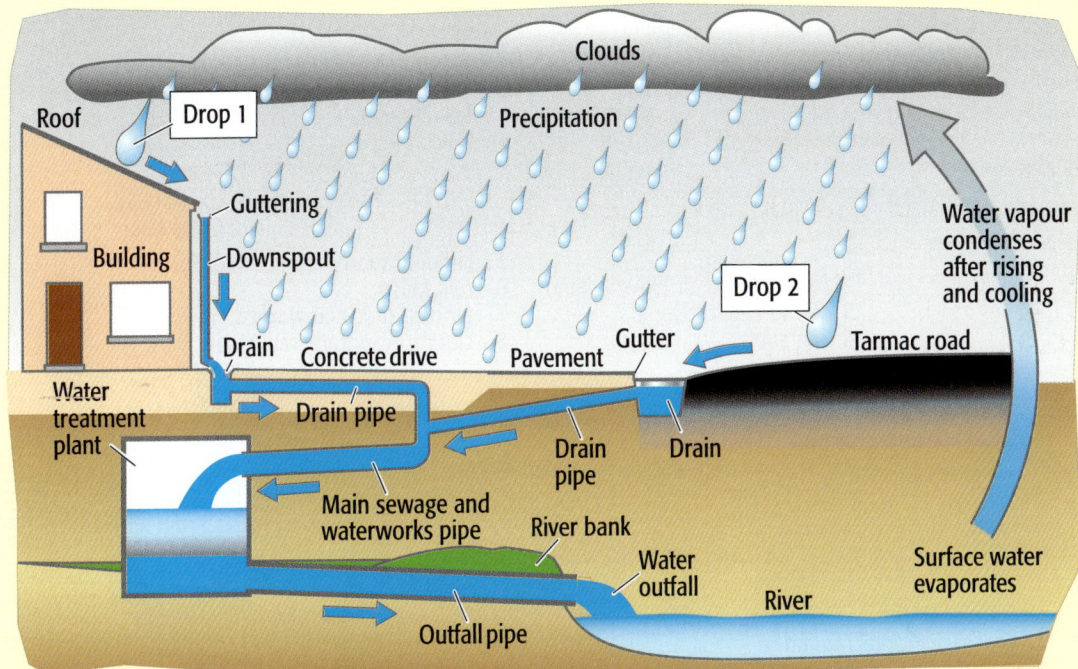

KEY FACTS

- People talk about sudden downpours of rain as cloudbursts – but clouds don't actually burst at all. People are simply describing what *seems* to happen when it suddenly starts to rain hard.
- Precipitation is only one of the terms people use when describing what the weather is like. Others are: temperature, wind speed, wind direction, amount of cloud cover and visibility (whether mist and fog affects how far people can see).
- The study of weather is called meteorology; meteorologists are people whose work is analysing weather information and producing weather forecasts.

• TOP TIPS •

Water vapour is usually invisible, but is often seen on the insides of windows in winter, when the air in a room is much warmer than that outside. The air next to the inside of the window cools down, can't hold as much water vapour and some of it then condenses on the pane of glass.

Rain, rain, go away...

If you've ever travelled across Europe, you might have noticed that fewer people seem to carry umbrellas as you go further inland. You would have to look quite hard to find any umbrella shops. This suggests that either it rains less in the east, or the people who live there aren't as bothered about getting wet. The first idea is true and the second is, of course, false.

All rain comes from clouds, and clouds only form where damp air rises and cools on its way up. This causes condensation to take place. So, to understand what *really* makes rain fall, we need to know what starts the air rising in the first place. There are three ways in which this can happen:

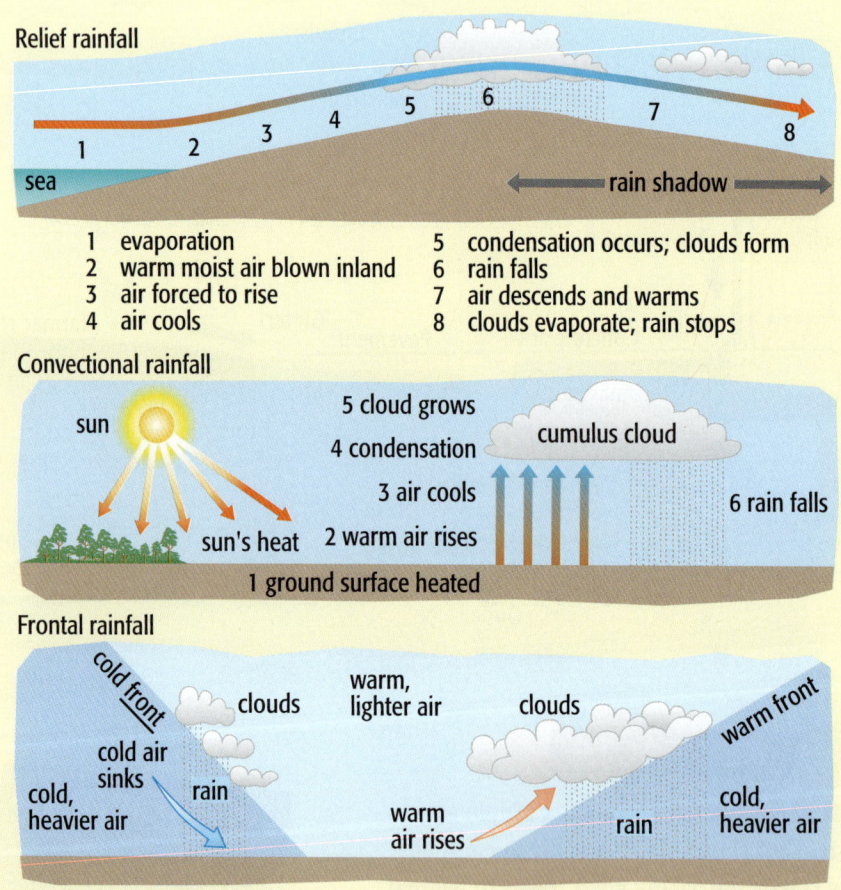

Relief rainfall

1. evaporation
2. warm moist air blown inland
3. air forced to rise
4. air cools
5. condensation occurs; clouds form
6. rain falls
7. air descends and warms
8. clouds evaporate; rain stops

Convectional rainfall

1. ground surface heated
2. warm air rises
3. air cools
4. condensation
5. cloud grows
6. rain falls

Frontal rainfall

In Western Europe, most rain is either relief (orographic) rainfall or frontal rainfall – because it is only warm enough for convectional rainfall to take place in the hottest summer months. Refer to your atlas for a relief map and a rainfall map of Western Europe.

Most of Western Europe is either on, or quite near to the sea. The main winds blow over Europe from the South West. These winds have travelled over 6000 km and collected a huge amount of water vapour from the Atlantic Ocean. The mountain regions of Europe receive the most rain. This is due to relief rainfall. The most westerly parts of Europe are much wetter than those further to the east. This is because the south westerly winds blow depressions (and their associated rainfall) into Europe from the North Atlantic Ocean. By the time the winds reach Eastern Europe, however, the air is much drier and so far less rain falls there.

Fill the gap

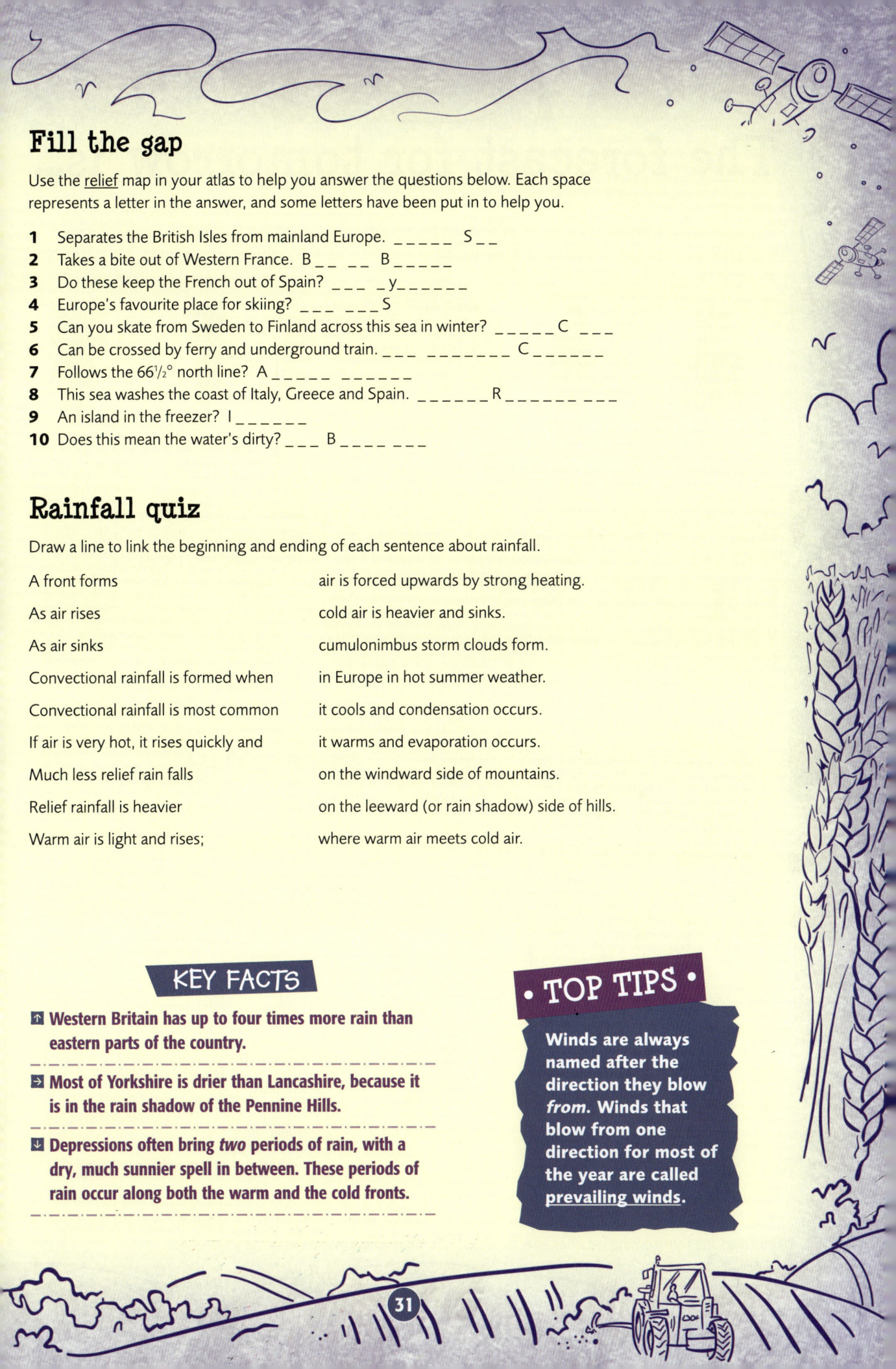

Use the relief map in your atlas to help you answer the questions below. Each space represents a letter in the answer, and some letters have been put in to help you.

1. Separates the British Isles from mainland Europe. _ _ _ _ _ S _ _
2. Takes a bite out of Western France. B _ _   _ _   B _ _ _ _ _
3. Do these keep the French out of Spain? _ _ _   _ y _ _ _ _ _ _
4. Europe's favourite place for skiing? _ _ _   _ _ _ S
5. Can you skate from Sweden to Finland across this sea in winter? _ _ _ _ _ C _ _ _
6. Can be crossed by ferry and underground train. _ _ _   _ _ _ _ _ _ _   C _ _ _ _ _ _
7. Follows the 66½° north line? A _ _ _ _ _   _ _ _ _ _ _
8. This sea washes the coast of Italy, Greece and Spain. _ _ _ _ _ _ R _ _ _ _ _ _ _ _ _
9. An island in the freezer? I _ _ _ _ _ _
10. Does this mean the water's dirty? _ _ _   B _ _ _ _   _ _ _

Rainfall quiz

Draw a line to link the beginning and ending of each sentence about rainfall.

A front forms	air is forced upwards by strong heating.
As air rises	cold air is heavier and sinks.
As air sinks	cumulonimbus storm clouds form.
Convectional rainfall is formed when	in Europe in hot summer weather.
Convectional rainfall is most common	it cools and condensation occurs.
If air is very hot, it rises quickly and	it warms and evaporation occurs.
Much less relief rain falls	on the windward side of mountains.
Relief rainfall is heavier	on the leeward (or rain shadow) side of hills.
Warm air is light and rises;	where warm air meets cold air.

KEY FACTS

- Western Britain has up to four times more rain than eastern parts of the country.
- Most of Yorkshire is drier than Lancashire, because it is in the rain shadow of the Pennine Hills.
- Depressions often bring *two* periods of rain, with a dry, much sunnier spell in between. These periods of rain occur along both the warm and the cold fronts.

• TOP TIPS •

Winds are always named after the direction they blow *from*. Winds that blow from one direction for most of the year are called prevailing winds.

The forecast for tomorrow is...

The weather plays an important part in all our lives because it changes very quickly. So, having an accurate weather forecast is really important to many groups of workers – as well as those who want to enjoy themselves out of doors.

OPEN cones were supposed to indicate dry weather

CLOSED cones were believed to show damp weather

"Red Sky at Night - Shepherds's Delight"
Red skies are caused by dust in the atmosphere; dust increases in dry air - so a red sky suggests dry weather is approaching

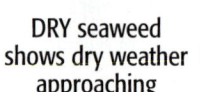
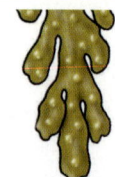

DRY seaweed shows dry weather approaching

WET seaweed that there is moist air approaching

These drawings show some of the traditional ways used in the past to predict the weather. However, to forecast weather accurately, we need detailed information about the conditions within the atmosphere. To gather the information they need, forecasters have networks of weather stations that are constantly monitoring atmospheric conditions and sending data back to their weather centres. Forecasters also collect information from ships, aircraft and weather balloons.

In the past, weather data had to be processed by the forecasters themselves, but this could take a long time and their predictions were often vague and unreliable. Today's powerful computers can quickly convert masses of information into the special weather maps that the forecasters use. The computers also compare this new information with their stored records of past weather patterns. When they find a good match between the two, they can predict what the weather is likely to be for the next four or five days.

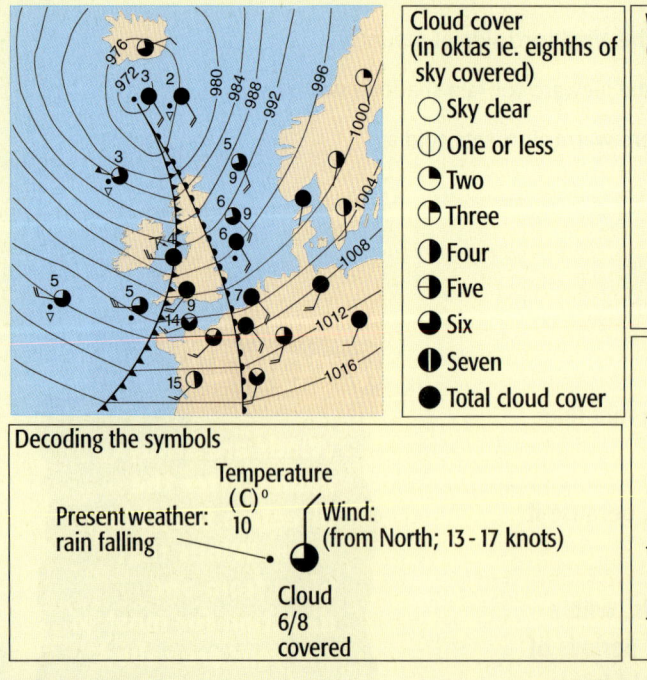

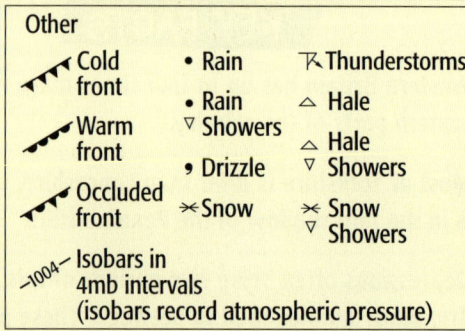

Satellite technology has improved both our understanding of how weather behaves and our ability to predict it. This is because satellites allow us to view the bigger picture and monitor what is happening globally. Forecasters can also see forthcoming weather events and predict their likely effects.

Weather wordsearch

The wordsearch below hides many groups of people who need accurate weather forecasts for their work or leisure activities.

```
C O A S T G U A R D S P O R T S P E O P L E
Q O I L R I G W O R K E R S E I L W E G H B
W T U S T E K R A M R E P U S I L D I A J A
E Y I N S D R A U G E F I L H C A E B R K L
S S O V C S A L P L S R O L I A S G H D E L
E R P B P I L O T S M M W E P R H O R E M O
A E E N Y D L I F E B O A T C R E W S N O O
S N A K U F S G O J N N S H A I R C V E U N
I A S F I S H E R M E N R H P U T M R R N I
D E D S I H D K I I B B E G T O U R I S T S
E L F S R E H C A E T V D F A H O U N E A T
L C G N I E F H U H V T L D I G I N M F I S
A W H M O G B G Y G R C I S N F J N F B N M
N O J W P H G M T A C S U N S D H E E F R O
D D K E P J G D I F X L B L G S G R D A E L
L N L R A S H N R L Z J Y K C T N S S R S I
A I Z T R K D S E D C H E N U B E D A M C L
D W X E S R E S C U E T E A M S E A O E U F
I U I T I K J A W S O G E B O D M U M R E G
E K C V D L K A Q S R E P E E K P O H S R E
S I E L E C T R I C I T Y W O R K E R S E D
R S R E L L E S C A E R C E C I Y T O D D S
```

• TOP TIPS •

TV weather forecasts use picture symbols, such as raindrops and snowflakes. These make it easier for us to see and remember what the weather is expected to be like. The <u>synoptic charts</u> that the forecasters themselves use are much more detailed and show cloud cover, wind speed and direction, as well as air pressure and weather fronts.

What's the weather today?

Choose any five groups of workers from your completed word search and then give a reason why accurate forecasts are important to each group.

Group of workers	Reasons for needing to know about the weather
1	
2	
3	
4	
5	

KEY FACTS

⬆ Land-based weather stations keep some of their recording instruments in a special wooden box called a Stevenson Screen. The box has slatted sides to allow air to flow freely through it. This means that air temperatures can always be taken in the shade.

➡ Wind direction is recorded by a wind vane and its speed by an anemometer.

⬇ Rainfall is collected in a measuring flask that is emptied daily.

⬆ The weather is so important to pilots and ships' captains that they have to study meteorology *and* pass exams in the subject.

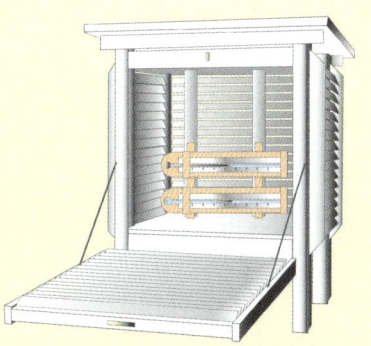
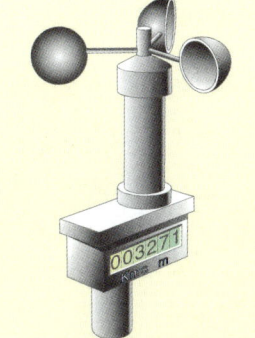

The Stevenson screen   A three-cup anemometer

Test your knowledge 4

1 List the four different kinds of precipitation.

....

(4 marks)

2 What is the other name for the Water Cycle? ....

(1 mark)

3 What must happen to the temperature of the air before clouds start to form?

....

(1 mark)

4 Write down the meanings of these key words:

Condensation   ....

Evaporation   ....

Precipitation   ....

(3 marks)

5 Put words in list into the corrrect boxes in the Water Cycle.

Surface run-off
Channel flow
Water table
Groundwater store

(3 marks)

6 Write your own description of how relief rainfall occurs. The first sentence has been written for you. Don't forget to mention the rain shadow area.

Heat from the sun evaporates sea water.

....

....

....

....

....

....
....
....
....

(5 marks)

7 Draw a simple sketch diagram to show convection rainfall. You need to add at least four labels to complete your drawing.

(4 marks)

8 How do computers help meteorologists to prepare accurate weather forecasts?

....
....
....

(3 marks)

9 Why are satellites so important for today's weather forecasters?

....
....
....

(2 marks)

10 Give four reasons why different groups of workers need to have accurate weather forecasts to help them in their jobs.

Reason 1: ....

Reason 2: ....

Reason 3: ....

Reason 4: ....

(4 marks)
(Total 28 marks)

Freezing in Finland; sweltering in Spain

Climates vary from place to place. Climate is *not* the same as weather but it can be described as being the average weather within a region. Meteorologists collect weather data over many years and calculate the average figures to get the climate for a typical year.

Many things influence what a particular climate is like. These are:

- distance from the Equator (latitude)
- the height of the land above sea level (altitude)
- proximity (how close something is) to the sea
- wind direction.

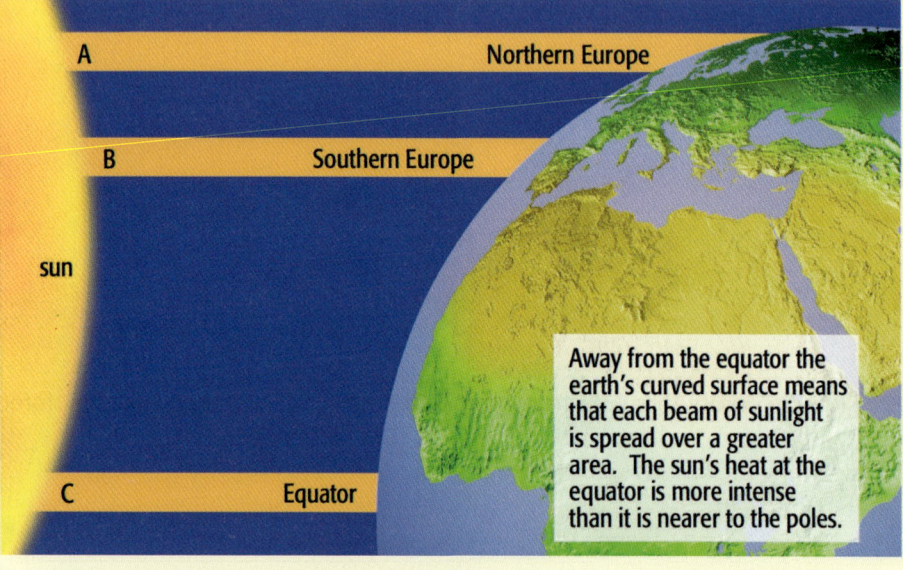

Away from the equator the earth's curved surface means that each beam of sunlight is spread over a greater area. The sun's heat at the equator is more intense than it is nearer to the poles.

Europe stretches from Crete (latitude 35°N) to Norway (71°N) and from Iceland (longitude 24°W) to the Ural Mountains in Russia at 60°E. Southern Europe is its hottest region but it is always very cold in the far north. This is because the sun's heat is not distributed equally across Europe's surface – the closer a place is to the Equator, the warmer it is.

The higher you climb up a mountain, the colder it becomes. Some parts of Europe, such as the Alps, are very mountainous and permanently snow-covered. Another effect of high land is that south-facing slopes get more sunshine and so are much warmer than any other slopes.

Europe is surrounded on three sides by sea – and this has a moderating effect on the coastal areas. Land heats up and cools down much faster than the sea. So, places near to a coast are cooler in summer but warmer in winter than inland places. This effect is known as Continentality.

Coastal climates are much wetter than those inland because the prevailing winds usually come from over the sea. Such winds are moist and bring rain. Further inland, climates are much drier, and in winter rain is replaced by snow because the temperatures are well below freezing.

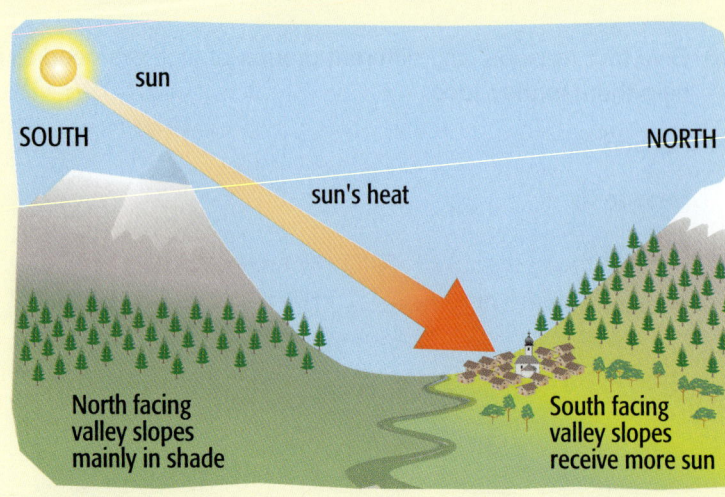

Climate jigsaw

Complete this word jigsaw by writing the groups of letters in the correct places on the puzzle. The blank squares and the five letters will help you to do this.

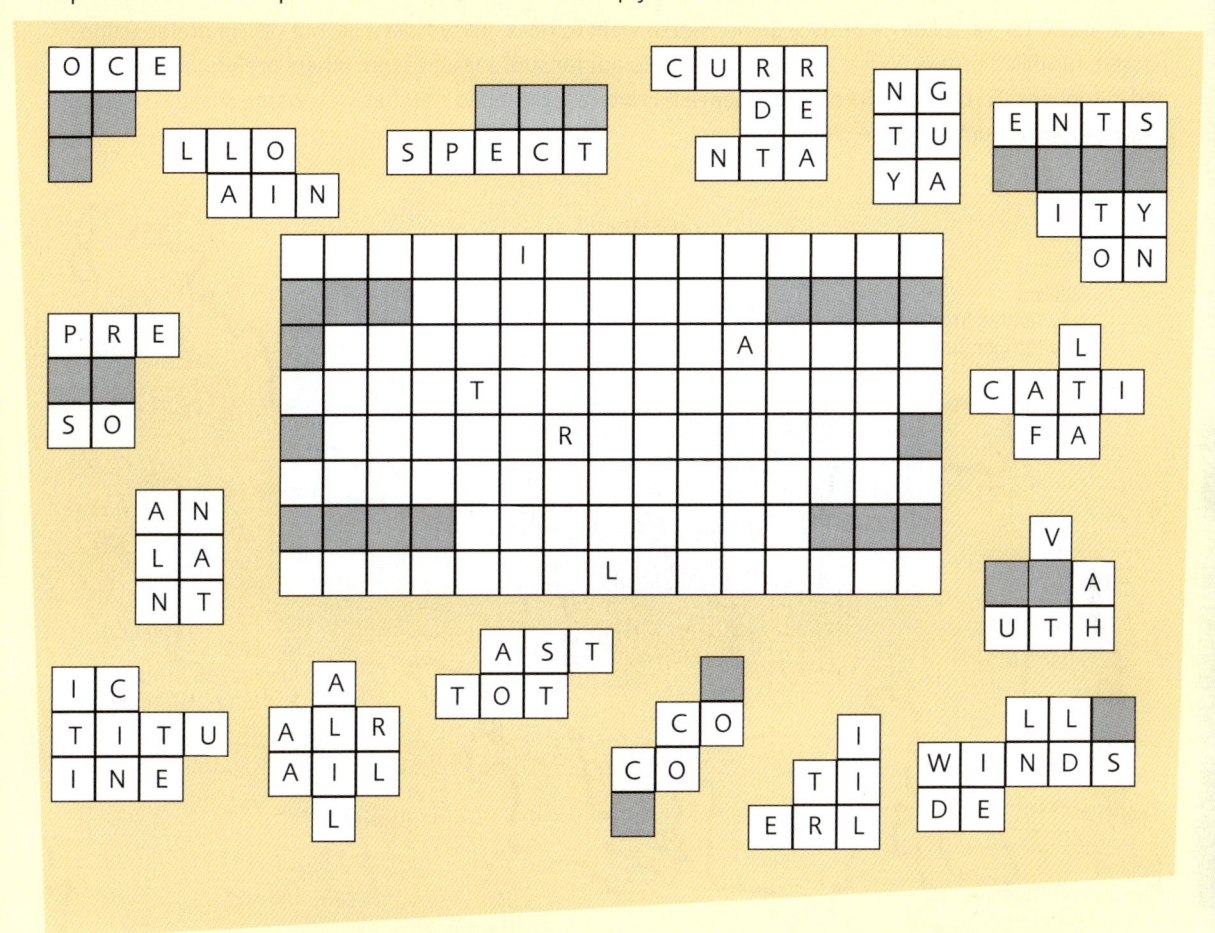

KEY FACTS

- Temperatures fall by 1°C for every 150 m of height. This means that the summits of the Alps, Europe's highest mountains, are about 30°C lower than the temperatures at the coast.

- 'Aspect' is the word used to describe the direction something faces. For example, classrooms with a southerly aspect get much more sunshine and are warmer. It's just the same with south-facing valley sides.

- Coastal climates are often affected by ocean currents. Europe's Atlantic coasts are much warmer in winter than those of North America. This is because the warm North Atlantic Drift current flows past them. Canada, however, has a very cold current that comes from the Arctic.

TOP TIPS

Coastal areas have a small <u>temperature range</u> (the difference between their summer maximum and winter low) due to the effects of the sea. However, places deep inside Europe have a much greater temperature range, because the summers are hot but their winters are extremely cold.

Do you ski or swim?

We all like to take a holiday – or two. Some people want to relax, away from it all, but others prefer action-packed, fun-filled breaks. While a number of people opt for sun, sea and sand, others prefer countryside, lakes and mountains. Fortunately, Europe has them all! From sun-drenched beaches with warm, shallow seas to snow-capped mountains – the choice is yours.

Iceland
July rainfall 51mm
July temperature 11°C

Lapland
July rainfall 66mm
July temperature 14°C

Moscow
July rainfall 81mm
July temperature 17°C

Ireland
July rainfall 64mm
July temperature 14°C

Ukraine
July rainfall 48mm
July temperature 22°C

Switzerland
July rainfall: varied
July temperature 19°C

Southern Spain
July rainfall 5mm
July temperature 25°C

Crete
July rainfall 3mm
July temperature 27°C

Climate contrasts

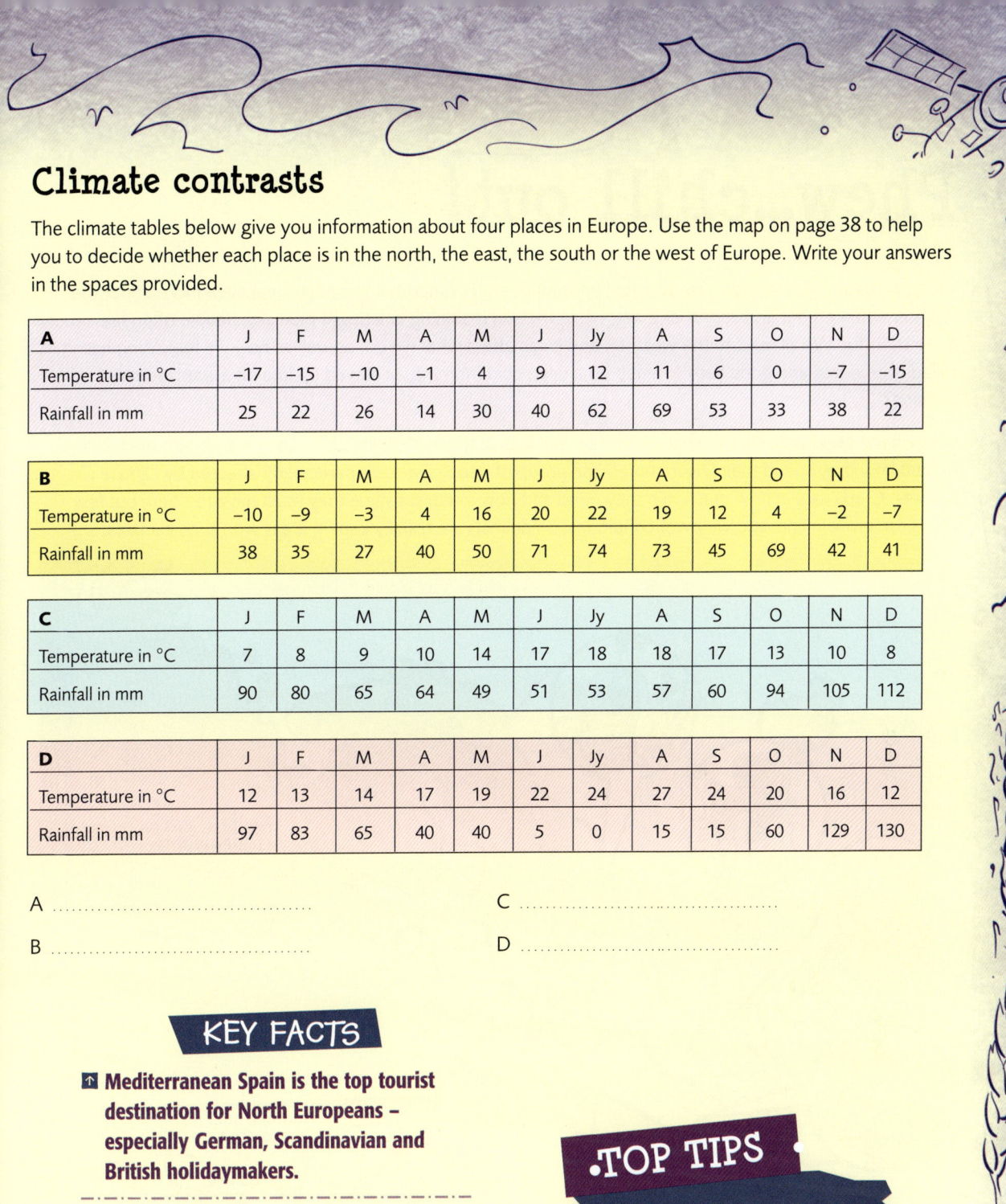

The climate tables below give you information about four places in Europe. Use the map on page 38 to help you to decide whether each place is in the north, the east, the south or the west of Europe. Write your answers in the spaces provided.

A	J	F	M	A	M	J	Jy	A	S	O	N	D
Temperature in °C	−17	−15	−10	−1	4	9	12	11	6	0	−7	−15
Rainfall in mm	25	22	26	14	30	40	62	69	53	33	38	22

B	J	F	M	A	M	J	Jy	A	S	O	N	D
Temperature in °C	−10	−9	−3	4	16	20	22	19	12	4	−2	−7
Rainfall in mm	38	35	27	40	50	71	74	73	45	69	42	41

C	J	F	M	A	M	J	Jy	A	S	O	N	D
Temperature in °C	7	8	9	10	14	17	18	18	17	13	10	8
Rainfall in mm	90	80	65	64	49	51	53	57	60	94	105	112

D	J	F	M	A	M	J	Jy	A	S	O	N	D
Temperature in °C	12	13	14	17	19	22	24	27	24	20	16	12
Rainfall in mm	97	83	65	40	40	5	0	15	15	60	129	130

A .... C ....
B .... D ....

KEY FACTS

- Mediterranean Spain is the top tourist destination for North Europeans – especially German, Scandinavian and British holidaymakers.
- The development of fast jet aircraft was a major boost to the tourist trade along Spain's Mediterranean coast.
- Many older people take extended winter holidays in Spain's *costas* (coasts) to avoid the cold, damp winters at home.
- The Alps are Europe's favourite 'winter playground' and attract thousands of skiers every year.

TOP TIPS

The Mediterranean climate has predictable hot, dry summers and mild winters with little rain. This guaranteed summer sunshine is one of the biggest attractions for families wanting a traditional beach holiday.

Phew...chill out!

When it's damp and cold, do you ever feel miserable, tired or moody? You might feel even more under the weather when it's hot and very sticky. Yet, when the sun is shining in a bright blue sky, people often feel much more cheerful. We all react to the weather, and it can affect what we do, as well as how we feel. Who hasn't rolled over in bed and gone back to sleep on a dark, cold morning, or stayed up late on a warm summer evening?

In much the same way, climate shapes how people live. It affects the kinds of houses they build, the jobs they do and how they spend their leisure time. One group of people who are particularly affected by climate are farmers. Crops vary in how much rain they need and how much sunshine they must have to ripen, but few crops can grow in cool and very wet conditions. So animals are usually kept in areas with such climates.

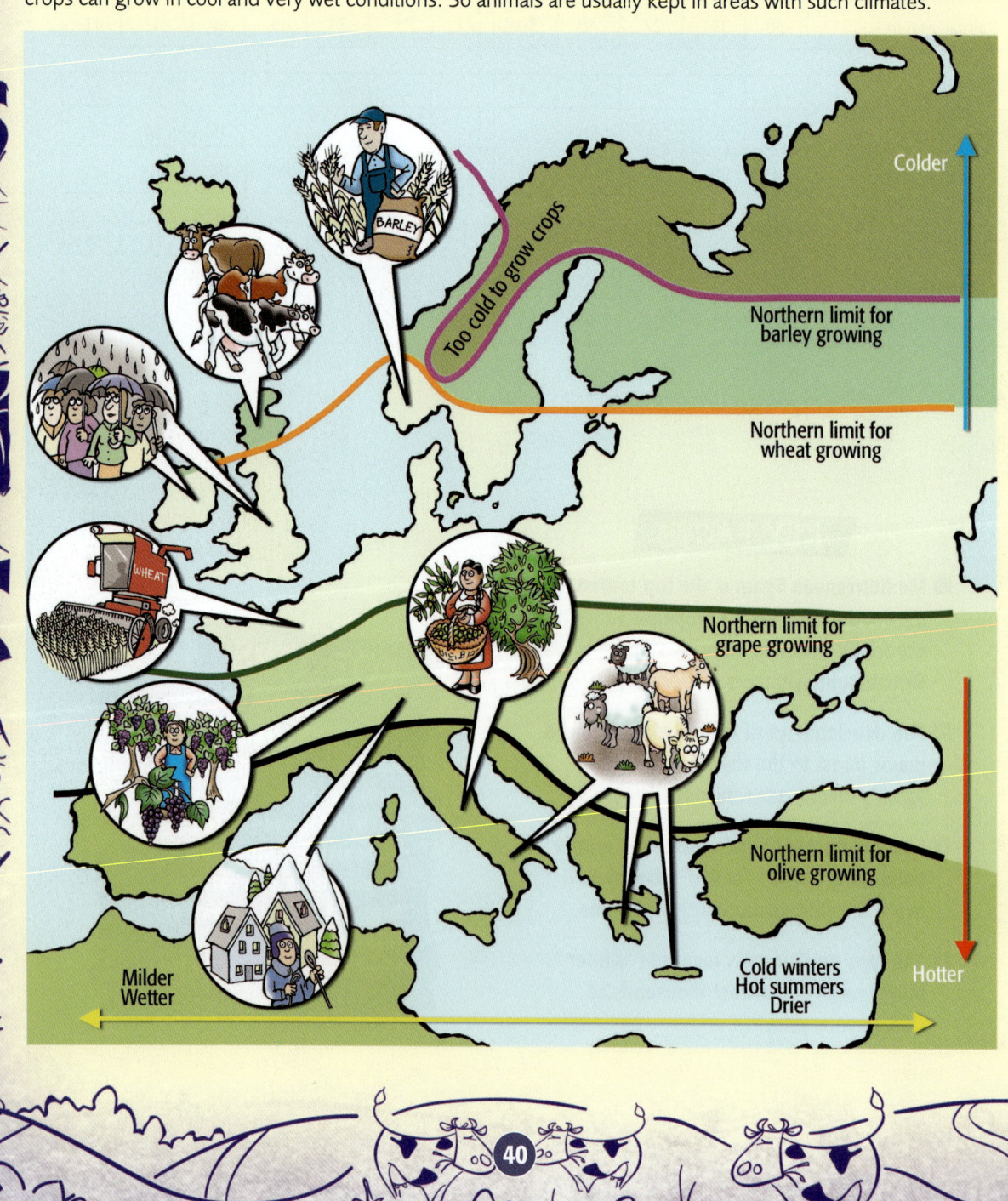

Climate crossword

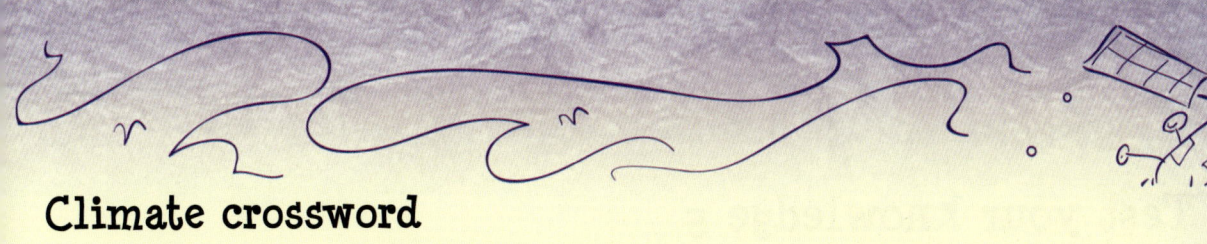

Use these clues and the information on page 40 to complete this 'skeleton crossword' about how climate affects people's lives.

Across

1. Used to stop heat loss at the top of a house (8, 3, 4)
3. Houses in hot countries have these to reflect the sun's heat (11, 5)
8. Keep a car warm in very cold winters (6, 6)
9. Crop grown in Spain, Italy and Greece to make cooking oil (6)
10. Europe's most important cereal crop (5)
12. Vehicle used to move snow off roads (4, 7)
15. *and* 17 Keeps all of the house warm (7) *and* (7)
16. Getting about on ice or water – using two pieces of wood! (6)
18. Alarm used to alert people about dangerous snow slides (9, 7)

Down

2. Motorised vehicle for travelling over snow (10)
4. Cuts heat loss through windows – *one* better than double-glazing! (6, 7)
5. Top feature of snow-proofed houses (5, 5)
6. Farmers do this on pasture land (4, 7)
7. Another cereal crop, grown in cooler, wetter areas (6)
10. Advice about how to keep warm when it's cold outside (4, 2, 4)
11. What to wear when it gets hot! (5, 8)
13. Hot steam rooms – popular in Scandinavia (6)
14. What you have to do to get grapes for winemaking (4, 5)

KEY FACTS

- Most plants can only grow when the temperature is over 6°C.
- Wheat grows best where the summers are hot and fairly dry. Oats and vegetables can grow in cooler and wetter areas.
- Dairy cattle are reared in areas that have lots of rain throughout the year; this produces rich pasture and therefore good quantities of milk.
- Winters become longer and colder the further north you go. Inside the Arctic Circle, there is no daylight at all in midwinter.

• TOP TIPS •

Climates vary a great deal across Europe. In the west, it is generally wet and mild. Eastern Europe, however, is much drier – with hotter summers and colder winters. In the far south, the Mediterranean region is hot and dry in summer (which makes it popular with holidaymakers) but cooler and wetter in winter. Summer droughts in the south and east of Europe cause water shortages, which make water rationing necessary.

Test your knowledge 5

1 Write a 'T' in the box to show which of these statements you think is true; use an 'F' for any that are false.

☐ *'Costa'* is the Spanish word for 'coast'.

☐ In winter, the coast of North America is much warmer than the Western European coast, on the opposite side of the Atlantic Ocean.

☐ Lines of *latitude* that pass through Europe have the letter N after their number of degrees.

☐ Plants stop growing when the temperature falls below 6°C.

☐ The North Atlantic Drift is a cold ocean current.

☐ Winds are always named after the direction they blow *from*.

(6 marks)

2 This map of Europe shows four very different climate areas. Write the letters A, B, C and D on the map to label each of these areas correctly.

A has hot, dry summers and mild, wet winters.

B has hot summers and freezing winters.

C has very short, cool summers and winter days that can have 24 hours of complete darkness.

D is Europe's wettest and mildest region.

Climate 1
Climate 2
Climate 3
Climate 4

(4 marks)

3 Cross out the wrong words shown in **bold** in these statements about the climate of Western Europe.

In the Mediterranean Region, summers have **almost no/lots of** rainfall in summer.

It becomes **colder/hotter** as you travel further inland in summer.

It becomes **colder/hotter** as you travel further inland in winter.

It becomes **colder/hotter** as you travel further north.

There is **less/more** rainfall as you travel further inland.

(5 marks)

4 Answer these questions, which are based on the coastal scene in the picture on page 43.

a) Describe the weather on this day

....
....
....

b) Is this picture showing a *summer* or a *winter* scene? ....

c) Write down whether you think this scene is in the north, south, east or western part of Europe.
....

(4 marks)

5 Pick the correct word from the box below to complete these sentences.

| altitude   aspect   latitude   prevailing winds   temperature range |

.... come from the same direction for most of the year.
.... is the difference between the highest summer and the lowest winter thermometer readings.
.... is the direction towards which something faces.
.... is the height of land above sea level.
.... tells you how far north a place is on a map.

(5 marks)

6 Write either *climate* or *weather* in each of the blanks spaces below.

The .... was so good this morning that we all decided to have a day out at the seaside. However, we didn't leave the house until we had watched the .... forecast on the TV. Luckily for us, the forecast was accurate and the .... later on was just how it had been described in the programme. The TV presenter had also talked a lot about the British ...., saying that it was usually much warmer in summer and that today's .... forecast was normal for this time of year.

(5 marks)
(Total 29 marks)

Hello, Brazil!

Mention Brazil, and most people immediately think about football, fiestas, forests and fun on the beaches! Our images of a place that we haven't yet visited come from what we have already seen, read and heard about them. This illustration shows some popular images of Brazil; does it match your own ideas about what Brazil is like?

Venezuela · **Guyana** · **Surinam** · **French Guiana** · **Columbia** · **Equator** · 0° · **Peru** · Manaus · Belém · Fortaleza · Rio Branco · Recife · **Bolivia** · Salvador · Brasília · Campo Grande · Belo Horizonte · Vitória · **Paraguay** · São Paulo · Rio de Janeiro · Tropic of Capricorn · Curitiba · 23½° · N · **Argentina** · Pôrto Alegre · **South Atlantic** · 0 Km 1,000

A   B   C

44

Images of Brazil

a) Three of the illustrations on page 44 have been labelled A to C. Study these images carefully, then describe what is shown in each of them. At the end of each description, show whether you think that this image shows Brazil to be a rich or a poor country.

A shows ....
....
                                                                   Poor/rich

B shows ....
....
                                                                   Poor/rich

C shows ....
....
                                                                   Poor/rich

b) Overall, do you think that the images on page 44 show you a rich or a poor country? ....

c) Choose any two of the images or details on the map on page 44 that you think accurately show life in Brazil, then two more that don't. The example shows you how to write your answers.

1 Much of northern Brazil is very hot because the Equator passes through it.

2 ....

3 ....

4 ....

5 ....

• TOP TIPS •

We call people's own ideas about a place their <u>mental images</u>. They're not always true to real life, but most people believe that they are!

KEY FACTS

⬆ The dense, tropical rainforest is teeming with vast numbers of animals, birds, reptiles and insects. It produces the famous Brazil nuts that we buy in the shops.

⬇ Football is *the* national sport. The members of its team, like Ronaldo, are national heroes and every youngster dreams of becoming as rich and famous as they are.

⬆ Fiestas are carnivals held in Brazil's biggest cities. They are an excellent excuse for dressing up, enjoying music and dancing in the streets. They are Brazil's own special 'festivals of fun'.

Reality strikes!

Many preconceptions that people have of Brazil are, in fact, true. It does have the world's largest tropical rainforest, football is its national sport and the climate – at least in the south east, where most people live – is ideal for lots of outdoor activities. But there are other aspects of life in Brazil that don't fit such images at all. These illustrations give you a more accurate picture of what Brazil is really like.

A

Key:
- Land over 1,000m
- Land over 500m
- Land 200–500m
- Land below 200m

Highland: A1 & A2 Guiana Highlands
  B Plateau of Mato Grosso
  C Brazilian Highlands
Lowland: D Amazon Basin
Rivers:
1 Negro
2 Amazon
3 Juruá
4 Purus
5 Madeira
6 Xingu
7 Araguaia
8 Tocantins
9 Paraná
10 São Fransisco
11 Paraná
12 Tapajós

B

Key:
- EQUATORIAL: Very hot all year. Much rain. Humid.
- SAVANNA: Hot wet summer. Very warm winter with drought.
- SEMI-DESERT: Hottest region. Littlerain. Rain very unreliable.
- TROPICAL: Hot all year. Rain all year.
- SUB-TROPICAL: Hot summer. Cooler winter. Moderate rainfall.

C

Cities: Belém, Fortaleza, Reclife, Salvador, Brasilia, Belo Horizonte, Sao Paulo, Curitiba, Rio de Janeiro, Porto Alegre

Key:
- Land used for mechanised commercial farming: crops include coffee, hobcicco, vines.
- Industrial areas and large cities. Mineral resources are found here too.
- Traditional subsistence and plantation farming. Cities are mainly ports.

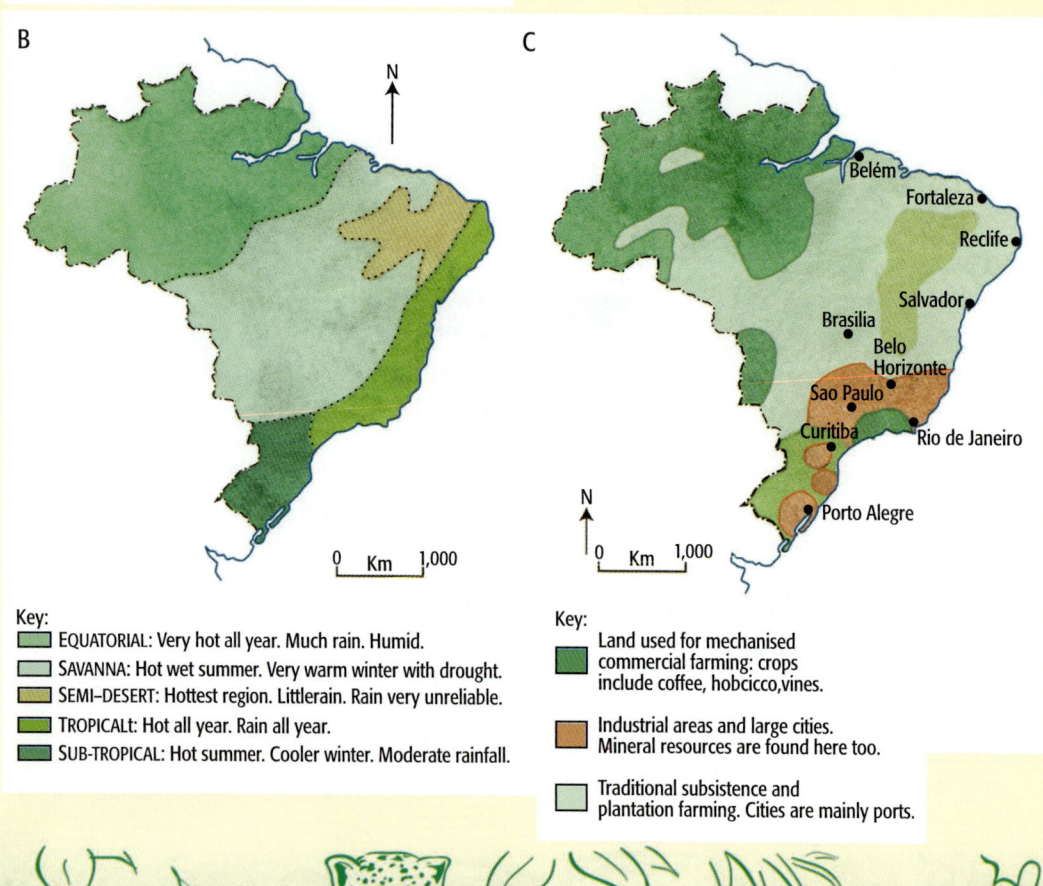

46

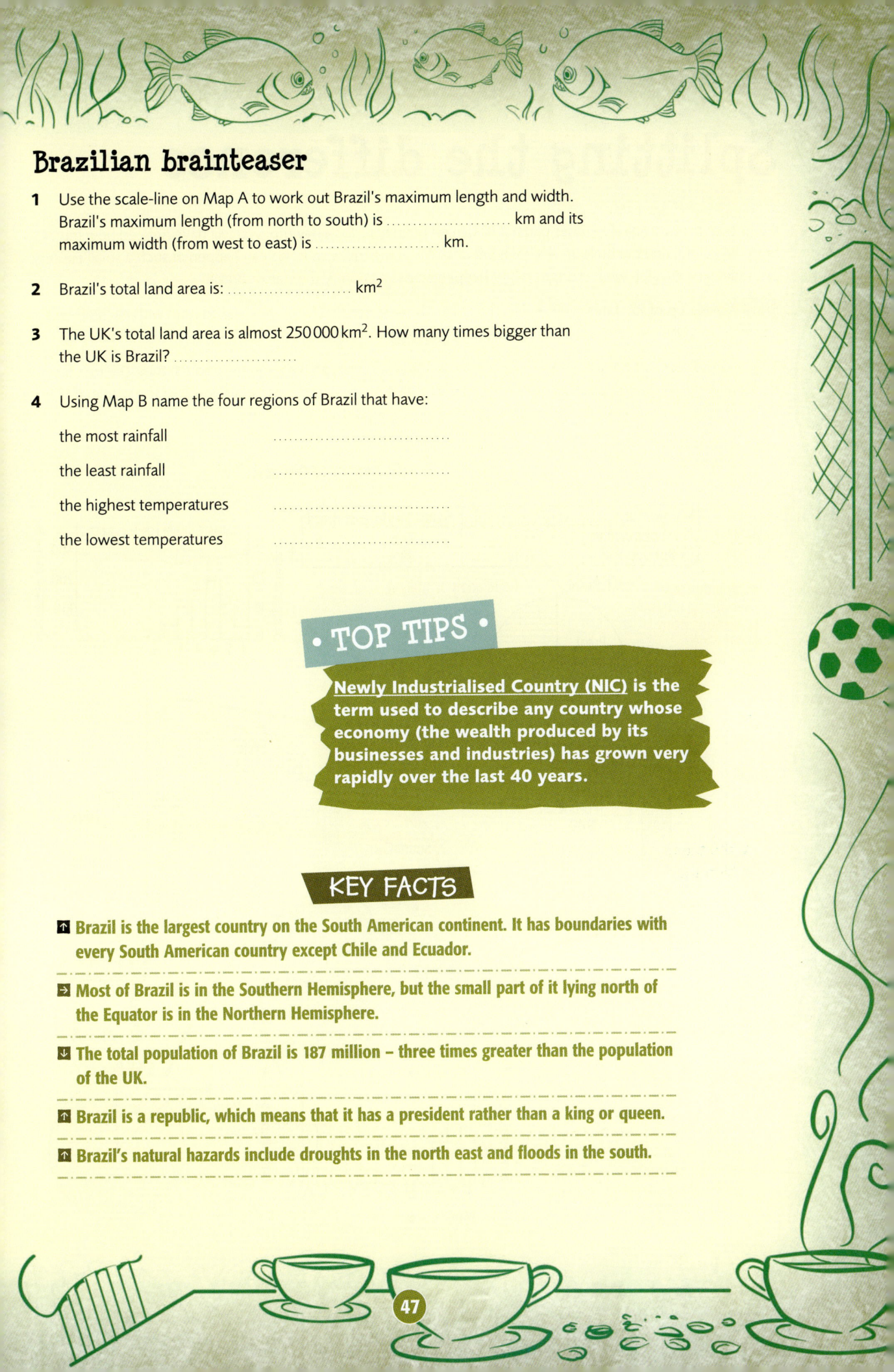

Brazilian brainteaser

1. Use the scale-line on Map A to work out Brazil's maximum length and width. Brazil's maximum length (from north to south) is .... km and its maximum width (from west to east) is .... km.

2. Brazil's total land area is: .... km²

3. The UK's total land area is almost 250 000 km². How many times bigger than the UK is Brazil? ....

4. Using Map B name the four regions of Brazil that have:

   the most rainfall ....

   the least rainfall ....

   the highest temperatures ....

   the lowest temperatures ....

• TOP TIPS •

Newly Industrialised Country (NIC) is the term used to describe any country whose economy (the wealth produced by its businesses and industries) has grown very rapidly over the last 40 years.

KEY FACTS

- Brazil is the largest country on the South American continent. It has boundaries with every South American country except Chile and Ecuador.

- Most of Brazil is in the Southern Hemisphere, but the small part of it lying north of the Equator is in the Northern Hemisphere.

- The total population of Brazil is 187 million – three times greater than the population of the UK.

- Brazil is a republic, which means that it has a president rather than a king or queen.

- Brazil's natural hazards include droughts in the north east and floods in the south.

Splitting the difference

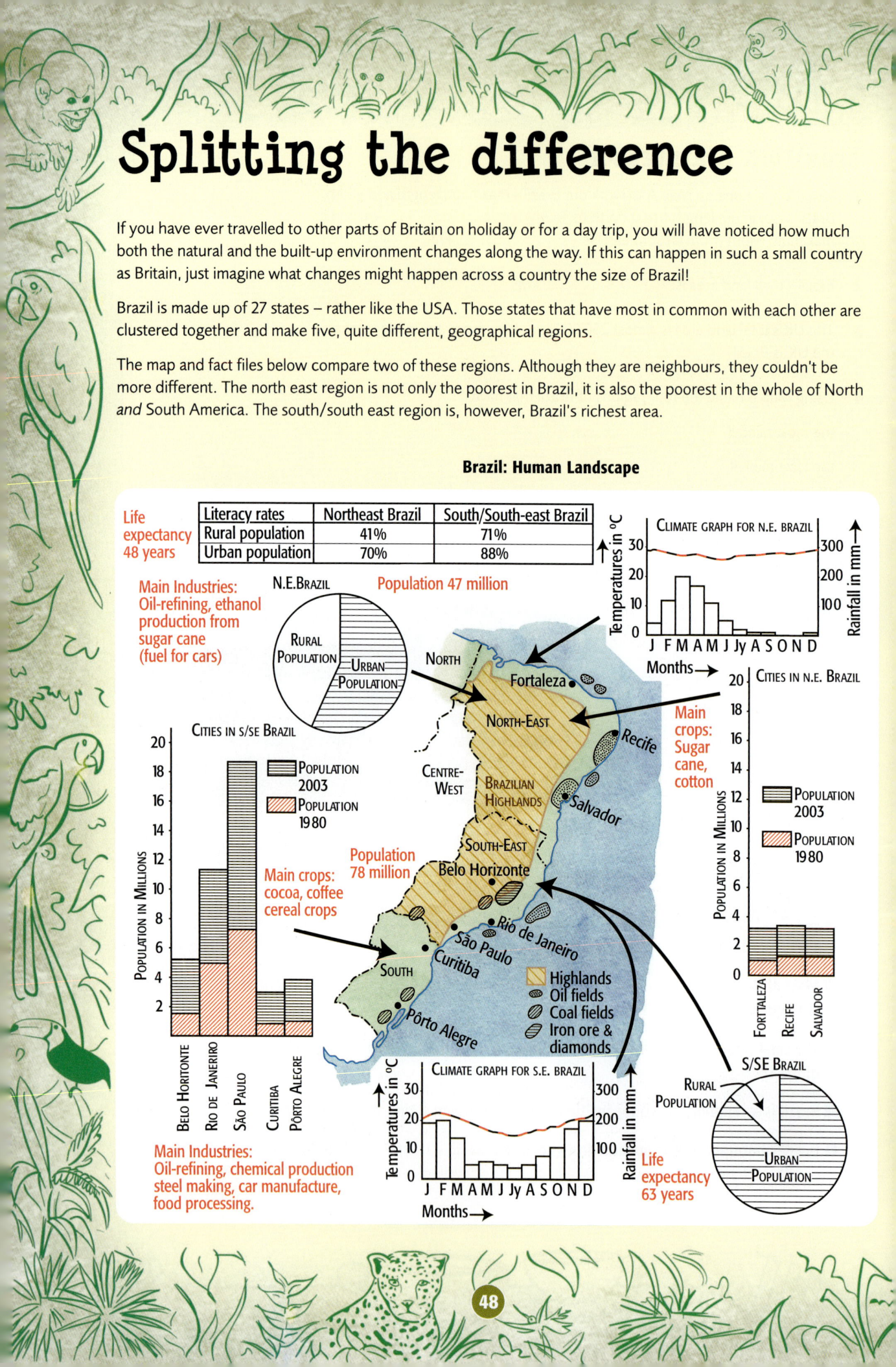

If you have ever travelled to other parts of Britain on holiday or for a day trip, you will have noticed how much both the natural and the built-up environment changes along the way. If this can happen in such a small country as Britain, just imagine what changes might happen across a country the size of Brazil!

Brazil is made up of 27 states – rather like the USA. Those states that have most in common with each other are clustered together and make five, quite different, geographical regions.

The map and fact files below compare two of these regions. Although they are neighbours, they couldn't be more different. The north east region is not only the poorest in Brazil, it is also the poorest in the whole of North *and* South America. The south/south east region is, however, Brazil's richest area.

Brazil: Human Landscape

Literacy rates	Northeast Brazil	South/South-east Brazil
Rural population	41%	71%
Urban population	70%	88%

N.E. Brazil
Life expectancy 48 years
Population 47 million

Main Industries: Oil-refining, ethanol production from sugar cane (fuel for cars)

Main crops: Sugar cane, cotton

S/SE Brazil
Population 78 million
Life expectancy 63 years

Main crops: cocoa, coffee cereal crops

Main Industries: Oil-refining, chemical production steel making, car manufacture, food processing.

Map key: Highlands, Oil fields, Coal fields, Iron ore & diamonds

Cities shown: Fortaleza, Recife, Salvador, Belo Horizonte, Rio de Janeiro, São Paulo, Curitiba, Pôrto Alegre

Regions: North, North-East, Centre-West, South-East, South, Brazilian Highlands

Brazilian life

1 Unjumble the letters in these circles to reveal information about agriculture in the north east and south/south east of Brazil. Write your answers in the table; some of these can be in both columns.

SUGARCANE   COFFEE   PLANTATIONS   COTTON

North east Brazil	South/South east Brazil

2 Read these three postcards that British students have received from their penfriends in Brazil. Decide if each penfriend lives in the north east or the south/south east region and write NE or S/SE in the space under each card.

A ....

Hi!
This is a picture of the finished HEP dam which my father helped build!

B ....

Guess what – this is where we'll be moving to next month!
Isn't it super?

C ....

Hi there! This is where my father and uncles work. They work hard in the fields as they have no machines to help them!

KEY FACTS

- It is mainly young people who migrate from the rural areas to the cities. This leaves a population of increasingly older people behind in the countryside.

- The newly-arrived find that there are few jobs for ill-educated, rural people. They can't find work or housing, so are forced to build flimsy shacks in slum areas known as favelas (shanty towns).

- Most favelas are on the edges of cities, a long way from the docks and factories that could provide employment for unskilled workers.

- Life in favelas is very difficult. Many have no clean water, sanitation or electricity and the high level of crime is a constant worry.

- Some migrants, who decide that moving was a big mistake, don't have enough money to return home.

Test your knowledge 6

1 Write one-word answers to these questions. Some of then have not been covered in this unit. See if you know the answers!

What is the national language of Brazil? ....

What is Brazil's capital city? ....

What is Brazil's national sport? ....

What is Brazil's unit of currency? ....

What kind of festivals are 'fiestas'? ....

What kind of fuel is found off the coast of south east Brazil? ....

What kind of natural hazard occurs in north east Brazil? ....

(7 marks)

2 Name these places shown on this map of Brazil.

Ocean 1: ....

Tropic line 2: ....

Range of mountains 3: ....

River 4: ....

River 5: ....

City 6: ....

City 7: ....

City 8: ....

(8 marks)

3 Half of these statements about Brazil are false. Put their letters in the spaces below, then rewrite their statements to make them read correctly.

A Most Brazilians live in cities.
B Mental images are what people think a place is like.
C The Equator is along the 0° line of latitude.
D The Brazilian flag has four colours: blue, green, red and white.
E The north east of Brazil is much richer than the South/South east.
F Most of Brazil lies in the Northern Hemisphere.
G Most of Brazil's largest cities are on or near to the coast.
H Brazil has 29 states, but only seven different geographical regions.

Statement .... is not true. It should say: ....

....

Statement .... is not true. It should say: ....

....

Statement .... is not true. It should say: ....

....

Statement .... is not true. It should say: ....

....

(4 marks)

4 These graphs show what the climate is like in three of Brazil's five regional areas. Decide which region each of the graphs belongs to, e.g. the north east, then give two reasons that helped you to make each decision.

A   **B**   **C**

Climate graph A is for the .... region.

Reason 1: ....

Reason 2: ....

Climate graph B is for the .... region.

Reason 1: ....

Reason 2: ....

Climate graph C is for the .... region.

Reason 1: ....

Reason 2: ....

(9 marks)

5 The drawing below shows a typical Brazilian favela. List four problems it shows about life for some of Brazil's poorest city dwellers.

Problem 1: ....

Problem 2: ....

Problem 3: ....

Problem 4: ....

(6 marks)
(Total 34 marks)

51

Brazil versus UK!

Brazilians are football fanatics. The British invented the game, and become upset when our teams are beaten, especially by France, Germany or Brazil!

The <u>developmental indicators</u> table below compares the facts and figures of Brazil and the UK; the pairs of photographs do the same for typical scenes in the two countries.

Developmental indicators	Brazil	UK
Population comparisons:		
Total population	187 million	60 million
Population age:		
0–14 years	26%	18%
5–64 years	68%	66%
65 years and over	6%	16%
Average age of population	28 years	39 years
Population growth per year	1%	0.3%
Birth rate per 1000 people	17%	11%
Death rate per 1000 people	6%	10%
Infant mortality rate per 1000 births	30%	5%
Life expectancy	72 years	78 years
Economic comparisons:		
Literacy rate	86%	99%
Average GDP per person	£4500	£16 500
Population living in poverty	22%	17%
Population working in:		
Primary industries	20%	1%
Secondary industries	14%	26%
Service industries	66%	73%
Land used for arable farming	7%	24%
Unemployment	12%	5%
Population with Internet access	8%	42%

Industry quiz

Primary industries get the natural resources we need. Secondary industries have factories that change these resources into goods we can buy. Service industries do things for us and give us a better life.

1. Look at the different kinds of work below and then write them in their correct columns in this table.

   steelmaking   mining   shipbuilding   policing   fishing   farming   oil refining   teaching   selling

Primary industries	Secondary industries	Service industries

2. Some other important terms were used in the table on the opposite page. Write each of the following terms at the start of its 'best-fit' meaning:

   arable farming   infant mortality rate   life expectancy   literacy   poverty   unemployment

   .... is growing crops.
   .... is how many years a person can expect to live.
   .... is not having a paid job.
   .... is the ability to read and write well.
   .... is the proportion of children who die before reaching four years of age.
   .... is when people don't have enough money eat and live properly.

3. Do the population comparisons in the table on page 52 suggest that Brazil is *richer* or *poorer* than the UK?
   ....

4. Do the economic comparisons in this table suggest that Brazil is a *richer* or *poorer* country than the UK?
   ....

KEY FACTS

- Infant mortality rates indicate a country's level of development. This is because they show important things about its standard of living.
- Life expectancy tells us about diet, hygiene and medical care.
- Literacy rates tell us about provision of teachers and learning resources. Education raises development levels and gives people the skills needed to get good jobs.
- The amount of arable land indicates a country's ability to grow food for its people.

TOP TIPS

GDP is a way of measuring how wealthy an average person in a country is. It is also a very useful way of comparing countries. Countries with a high GDP are called More Economically Developed Countries (MEDCs); poor countries with a low GDP are called Less Economically Developed Countries (LEDCs). Brazil, which is between the two, is a Newly Industrialised Country (NIC).

Back to the future!

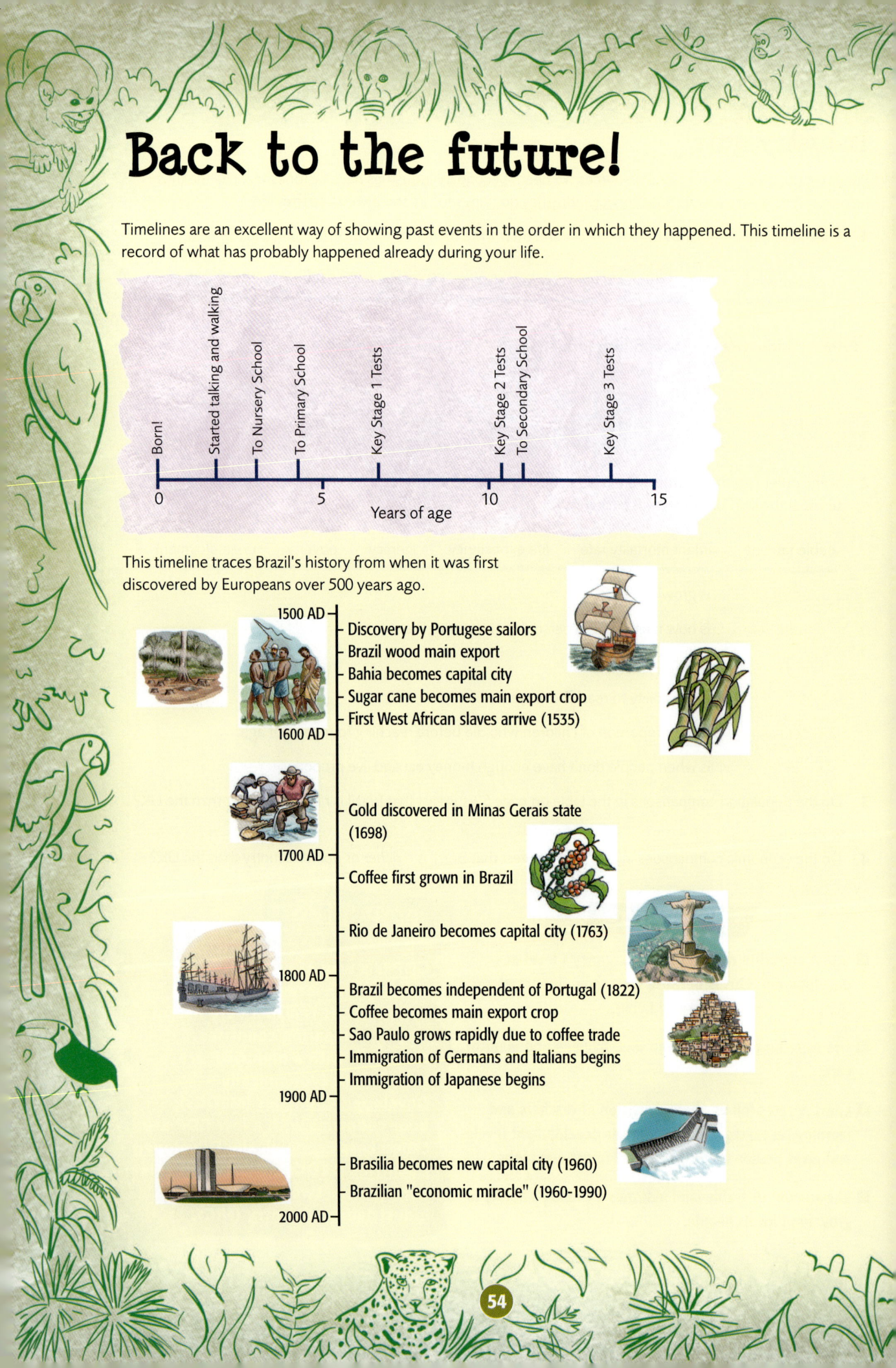

Timelines are an excellent way of showing past events in the order in which they happened. This timeline is a record of what has probably happened already during your life.

- 0 — Born!
- Started talking and walking
- To Nursery School
- To Primary School
- 5 — Key Stage 1 Tests
- 10 — Key Stage 2 Tests
- To Secondary School
- 15 — Key Stage 3 Tests

Years of age

This timeline traces Brazil's history from when it was first discovered by Europeans over 500 years ago.

1500 AD
- Discovery by Portugese sailors
- Brazil wood main export
- Bahia becomes capital city
- Sugar cane becomes main export crop
- First West African slaves arrive (1535)

1600 AD

- Gold discovered in Minas Gerais state (1698)

1700 AD
- Coffee first grown in Brazil
- Rio de Janeiro becomes capital city (1763)

1800 AD
- Brazil becomes independent of Portugal (1822)
- Coffee becomes main export crop
- Sao Paulo grows rapidly due to coffee trade
- Immigration of Germans and Italians begins
- Immigration of Japanese begins

1900 AD

- Brasilia becomes new capital city (1960)
- Brazilian "economic miracle" (1960-1990)

2000 AD

Brazilian crossword

Complete this skeleton crossword about Brazil's history by answering the clues below it. When you have finished it, the name of a major city and port in Brazil will be revealed.

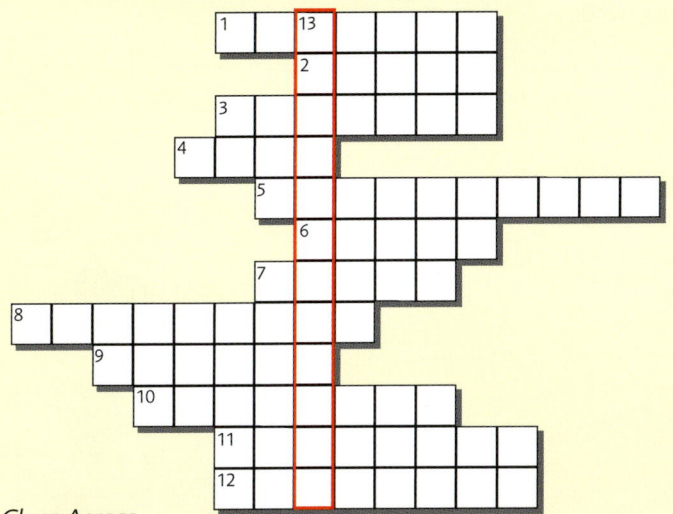

TOP TIPS

Most South American countries have suffered major civil wars and other forms of violent conflict since becoming independent. Brazil, however, has not. One possible reason for this is that Brazil was the only country on the South American continent to be ruled by the Portuguese instead of the Spanish, who were far more ruthless with the people they had conquered.

Clues Across

1. One of the countries from which migrants arrived at the end of the 19th century.
2. Another country from which these migrants moved.
3. Huge deposits of this helped set up Belo Horizonte's iron and steel industry.
4. Discovered in Minas Gerais in 1698.
5. Origin of Brazil's slaves.
6. Where the early 20th century slaves arrived from.
7. The very first capital city.
8. Brazil's first export crop.
9. Beverage crop, introduced to Brazil in the 18th century.
10. Capital city – but only since 1960.
11. Brazil gained independence from this country in 1822.
12. The city that grew rapidly because of coffee exports.

Which important city is now revealed at 13 Down?

KEY FACTS

- There were between three and five million Indians in Brazil before 1500. Now there are only 16 000. There are many reasons for this very steep decline in numbers:
  - Many Indians were used as slaves by European settlers and died as a result of the hard work and harsh treatment.
  - The European settlers and traders brought diseases against which the Brazilian Indians had no bodily defences. Many died of chickenpox, measles and scarlet fever.
  - Deforestation has taken place in order to obtain valuable timber and clear the land for other uses. Doing this has, however, deprived many Indians of their homes and traditional tribal hunting grounds.

- All the ethnic groups of Brazil usually get on well with each other, perhaps because most of them are immigrants themselves! This pie chart shows how Brazil's population is divided between its three main ethnic groups.

Onward and upward?

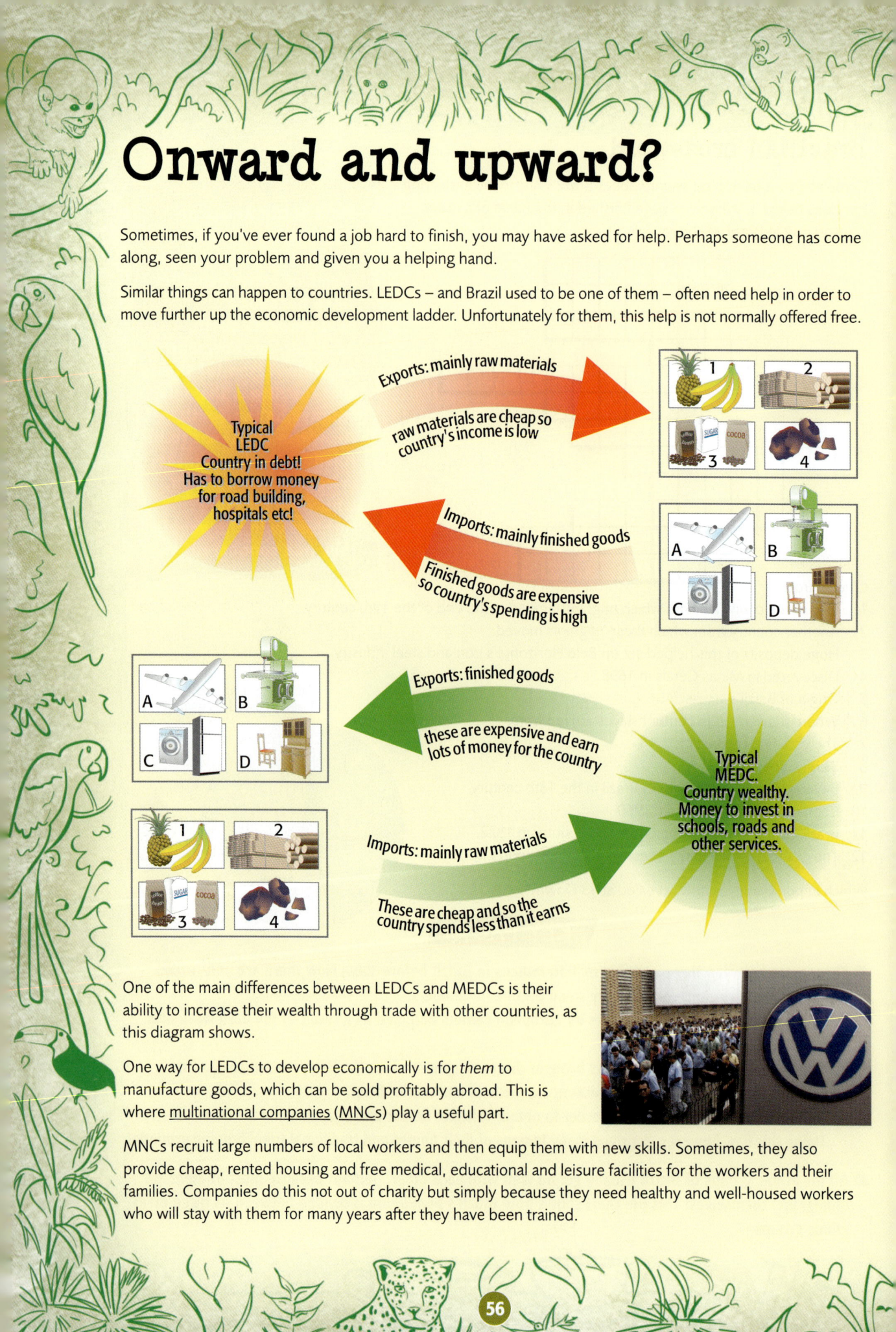

Sometimes, if you've ever found a job hard to finish, you may have asked for help. Perhaps someone has come along, seen your problem and given you a helping hand.

Similar things can happen to countries. LEDCs – and Brazil used to be one of them – often need help in order to move further up the economic development ladder. Unfortunately for them, this help is not normally offered free.

Typical LEDC Country in debt! Has to borrow money for road building, hospitals etc!

Exports: mainly raw materials
raw materials are cheap so country's income is low

Imports: mainly finished goods
Finished goods are expensive so country's spending is high

Exports: finished goods
these are expensive and earn lots of money for the country

Imports: mainly raw materials
These are cheap and so the country spends less than it earns

Typical MEDC. Country wealthy. Money to invest in schools, roads and other services.

One of the main differences between LEDCs and MEDCs is their ability to increase their wealth through trade with other countries, as this diagram shows.

One way for LEDCs to develop economically is for *them* to manufacture goods, which can be sold profitably abroad. This is where multinational companies (MNCs) play a useful part.

MNCs recruit large numbers of local workers and then equip them with new skills. Sometimes, they also provide cheap, rented housing and free medical, educational and leisure facilities for the workers and their families. Companies do this not out of charity but simply because they need healthy and well-housed workers who will stay with them for many years after they have been trained.

Import/export quiz

1. Complete this 'word jigsaw' by writing the groups of letters in the correct places on the puzzle.

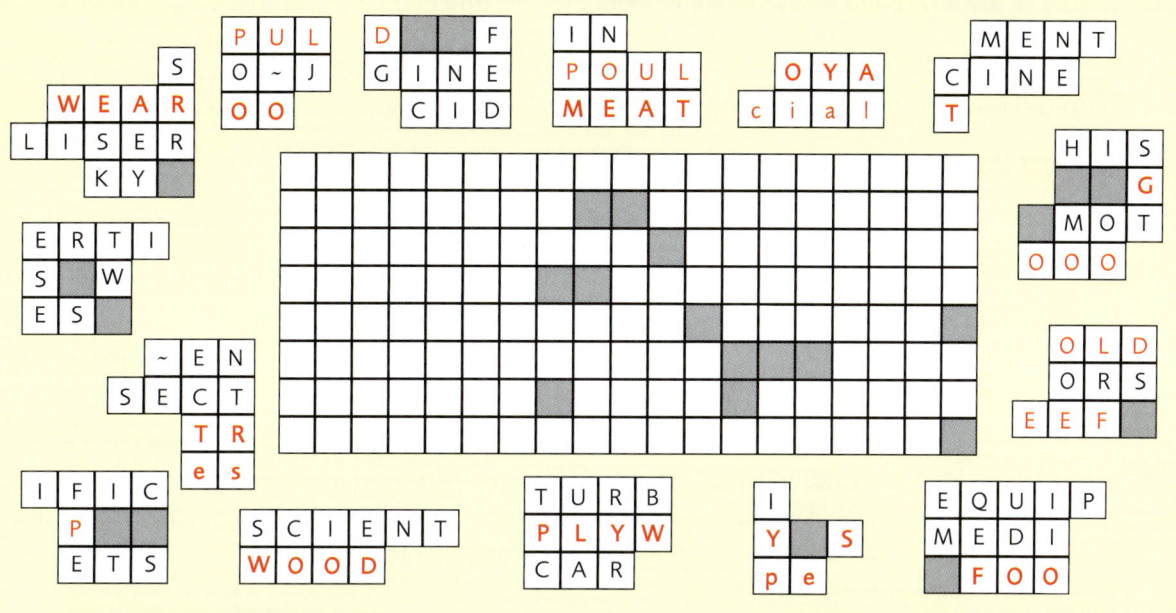

2. This puzzle used two different colours – one for Brazil's exports to the UK and one for its imports from the UK. Use the information in your completed puzzle to help you finish the table below.

Brazil's exports to the UK	Brazil's imports from the UK

• TOP TIPS •

One major disadvantage of Brazil's push for rapid economic development has been large-scale clearance of the Amazon rainforest. So far, deforestation has been seen as a quick way for Brazil to earn money, because its mahogany and teak hardwoods have been used for high-quality furniture and buildings in MEDCs.

KEY FACTS

- Most multinational companies have their headquarters in MEDCs like Japan, the USA and the UK, but many of their factories are in less well-off countries such as Brazil. The workers' wages in LEDCs are much lower so the companies can sell their goods at a higher profit.

- Deforestation has increased in recent years due to:
    - the mining of iron ore and other valuable minerals from under the rainforest
    - new roads and railways that have been built through the forest
    - hydroelectricity generating plants that have dammed rivers and created huge reservoirs behind them.

- Deforestation is a key factor in global warming because the forests recycle carbon dioxide. Less trees results in an increase in CO_2 levels. This is believed to be a major cause of warming of the atmosphere.

Test your knowledge 7

1 Write a 'T' by any of the following statements that are true and an 'F' for those that are false.

☐ Brazil's population growth is faster than that of the UK.

☐ Brazil has a higher birth rate than the UK, and a higher infant mortality rate.

☐ Most Brazilians don't live as long as people in the UK.

☐ Brazilians receive a better basic education than students in the UK.

☐ Brazil's total population is about three times greater than that of the UK.

☐ Brazil has a smaller *proportion* of older people than the UK.

(6 marks)

2 Which *economic* indicators have these meanings?

.... shows how effective schools are in teaching people how to read and write.

.... shows how rich or poor an average person in a country is.

.... shows whether people have an adequate standard of care *very* early in life.

.... shows whether people have enough money to provide themselves with adequate food, clothing and housing.

.... shows how many people are able to get onto web sites using computers in their home or workplace.

(5 marks)

3 Put these events in Brazil's history in their correct 'century box' in the table below:

> Brazil becomes independent of Portugal   Brasilia becomes the new capital city
> 'Brazilian' Economic Miracle;   Coffee becomes the main export crop
> Coffee first grown in Brazil   Discovery by Portuguese sailors
> First West African slaves arrive   Gold discovered in Minas Gerais State
> Immigration of Germans and Italians begins   Rio de Janeiro becomes capital city

Century	Events happening in this century
Sixteenth	
Sixteenth	
Seventeenth	
Eighteenth	
Eighteenth	
Nineteenth	
Nineteenth	
Nineteenth	
Twentieth	
Twentieth	

(10 marks)

4 Put these three groups of countries in their correct order of increasing wealth: *Less economically developed countries; More economically developed countries; Newly industrialised countries.*

.... (poorest countries)

....

.... (richest countries)

(3 marks)

5 Briefly describe any two reasons why the number of native Indian people in Brazil has dropped so rapidly.

First reason: ....

....

Second reason: ....

....

(2 marks)

6 Insert the dates of these three important events in the history of Brazil.

The year when Brazil was discovered by the Portuguese. ....

The year when São Paulo started to expand because of the coffee grown near to it. ....

The year when Brasilia was officially opened as Brazil's new capital city. ....

(3 marks)

7 List these types of work by their correct industry groups:

| airline pilot | coal miner | forestry worker | oil refinery worker | shipbuilder | teacher |

Primary industries: ....

Secondary industries: ....

Service industries: ....

(3 marks)

8 These drawings show the types of goods that are traded between Brazil and the UK. Write *Brazil* or *the UK* by each item to show which country imports them.

....

(3 marks)

9 In which kinds of countries (LEDCs or MEDCs) do multinational companies have:

their headquarters? ....

most of their factories? ....

(2 marks)

10 What is the other name used for multinational companies?

....

(1 mark)
(Total 38 marks)

Patterns on the planet

According to this Howler Monkey, the weather in the tropical rainforest is the same every day!

'Hello! I want to h-o-w-l about the weather where I live! Yesterday started hot and sticky. It was over 30°C all day and it poured down early in the afternoon. There was a terrific thunderstorm at the same time! The evening was clear and the sun shone brightly. Today, there was bright sunshine in the morning and it has been very hot since dawn but heavy rain and thunder started about 2 pm. Guess what the forecast for tomorrow will be like!!!'

The world's surface is covered by patterns and some of the largest of these are made by its natural regions. For example, the climate of a place depends on how far it is from the Equator and the nearest ocean, and the type of climate affects the plants and animals that can live there. Regions with similar climates and plants are called biomes. Four examples of these are: coniferous forest, deciduous forest, hot desert and savanna grassland. Most biomes cover very large areas.

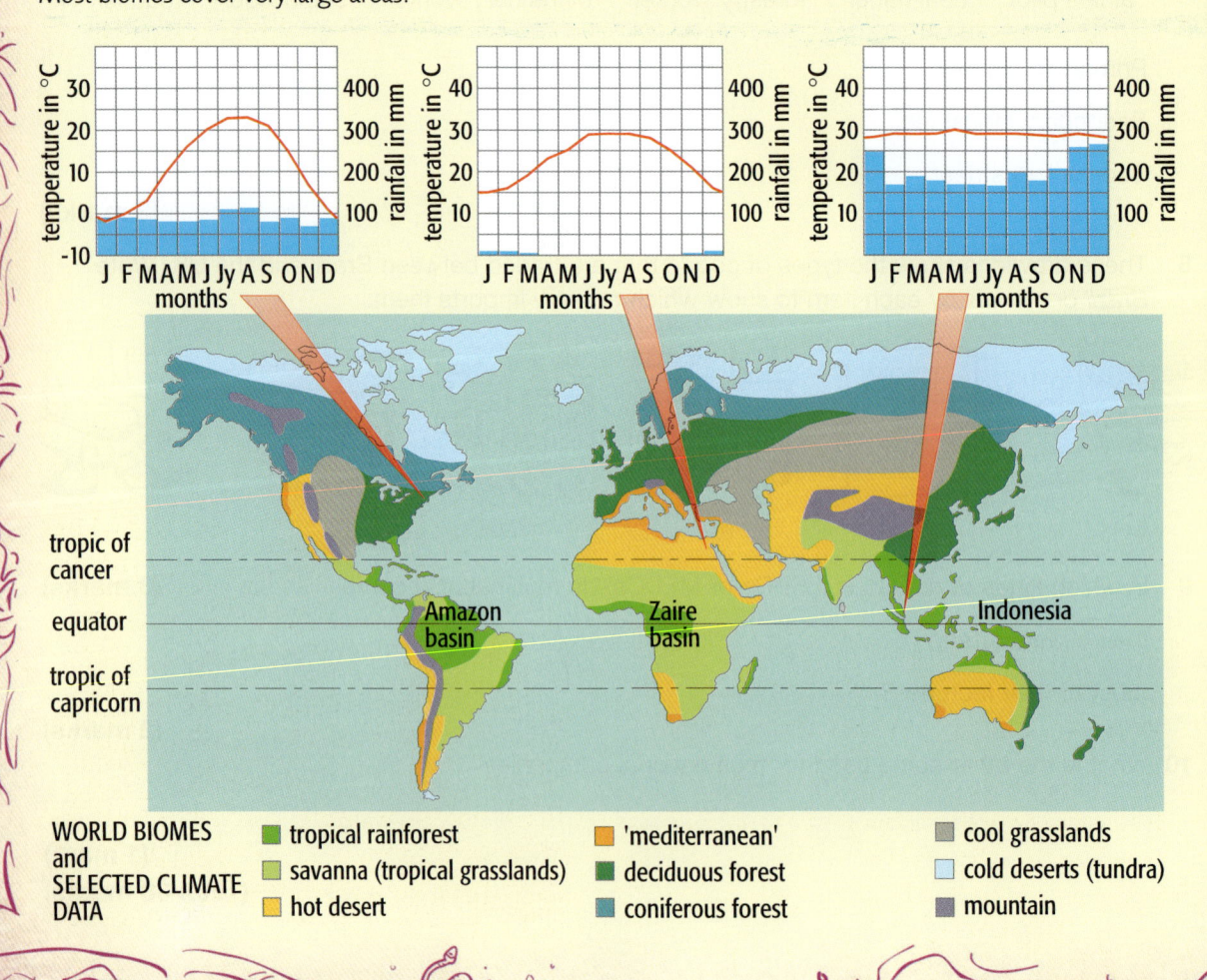

WORLD BIOMES and SELECTED CLIMATE DATA

- tropical rainforest
- savanna (tropical grasslands)
- hot desert
- 'mediterranean'
- deciduous forest
- coniferous forest
- cool grasslands
- cold deserts (tundra)
- mountain

Tree adaptation

Draw a straight line to link each adaptation label to an appropriate feature on the correct tree.

Acacia

Fir/cone

Conical shape/flexible branches allow snow to slide off.

Deciduous leaves drop in dry season.

Long tap roots can reach water table deep underground.

Roots are shallow because lower soil layers are permanently frozen.

Roots spread outwards to get water from a wide area.

Seeds are protected against cold within cones.

Small waxy leaves reduce loss of water.

Thick bark gives protection against cold weather.

Thick bark protects tree from fire damage in hot weather.

Thin, wax-covered leaves called needles protect tree from frostbite and reduce water loss in summer.

KEY FACTS

- The hottest climates are found between the Tropics of Cancer and Capricorn.
- Savanna grassland biomes have trees as well as grass cover. Some of these trees, such as baobab trees, store water in their huge, spongy trunks.
- Trees in deciduous forest biomes shed their leaves for winter to prevent frost damage and to reduce water loss.

TOP TIPS

Plants and trees adapt to drought conditions in three ways:

1 they have long taproots to reach more water

2 they are able to store water inside their stems and trunks

3 they are also developed to prevent (much) water loss through evaporation.

Welcome to our habitat

YOU are a member of an animal species called *Homo Sapiens*. This is a very special – in fact unique – species, simply because it can adapt to living on any part of the Earth's surface. For example, you can wear different clothes to be comfortable in both summer and winter. Most species can only survive in places with a particular set of natural conditions, such as climate and vegetation. Amazingly, over 50% of the world's plants and animals have adapted to living in the tropical rainforests. This drawing shows how rainforest plants and some of its animals have adapted and interact with each other.

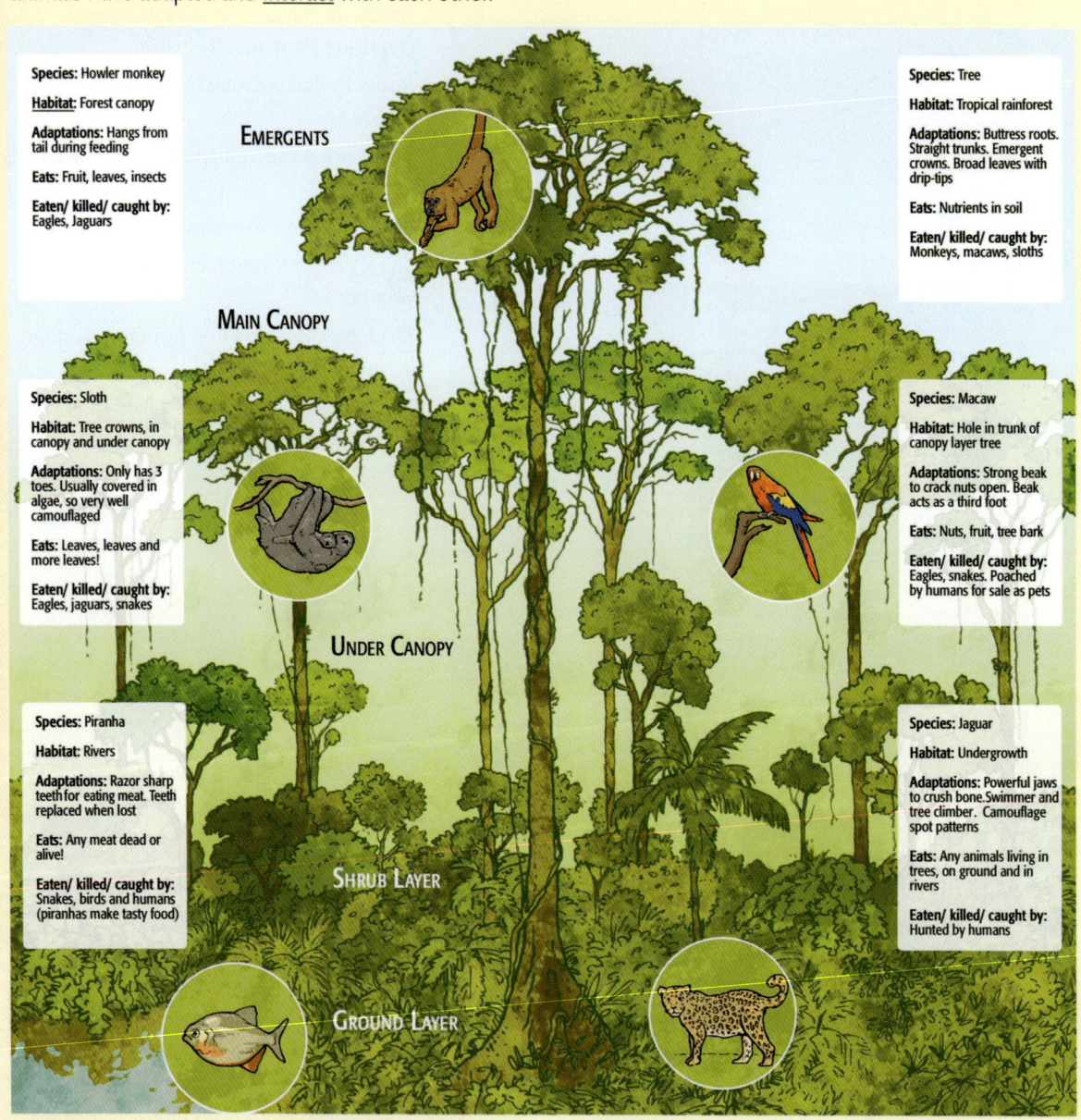

EMERGENTS

Species: Howler monkey
Habitat: Forest canopy
Adaptations: Hangs from tail during feeding
Eats: Fruit, leaves, insects
Eaten/ killed/ caught by: Eagles, Jaguars

Species: Tree
Habitat: Tropical rainforest
Adaptations: Buttress roots. Straight trunks. Emergent crowns. Broad leaves with drip-tips
Eats: Nutrients in soil
Eaten/ killed/ caught by: Monkeys, macaws, sloths

MAIN CANOPY

Species: Sloth
Habitat: Tree crowns, in canopy and under canopy
Adaptations: Only has 3 toes. Usually covered in algae, so very well camouflaged
Eats: Leaves, leaves and more leaves!
Eaten/ killed/ caught by: Eagles, jaguars, snakes

Species: Macaw
Habitat: Hole in trunk of canopy layer tree
Adaptations: Strong beak to crack nuts open. Beak acts as a third foot
Eats: Nuts, fruit, tree bark
Eaten/ killed/ caught by: Eagles, snakes. Poached by humans for sale as pets

UNDER CANOPY

Species: Piranha
Habitat: Rivers
Adaptations: Razor sharp teeth for eating meat. Teeth replaced when lost
Eats: Any meat dead or alive!
Eaten/ killed/ caught by: Snakes, birds and humans (piranhas make tasty food)

Species: Jaguar
Habitat: Undergrowth
Adaptations: Powerful jaws to crush bone. Swimmer and tree climber. Camouflage spot patterns
Eats: Any animals living in trees, on ground and in rivers
Eaten/ killed/ caught by: Hunted by humans

SHRUB LAYER

GROUND LAYER

Plants and animals that live and interact together form a community. Communities interact with the non-living parts of their environment (soil, air and climate) to form an ecosystem. When lots of similar ecosystems occupy a very large part of the world with a similar climate, they are known as a biome.

Gold run

Follow any route across the Blockbuster board, using the clues below it.

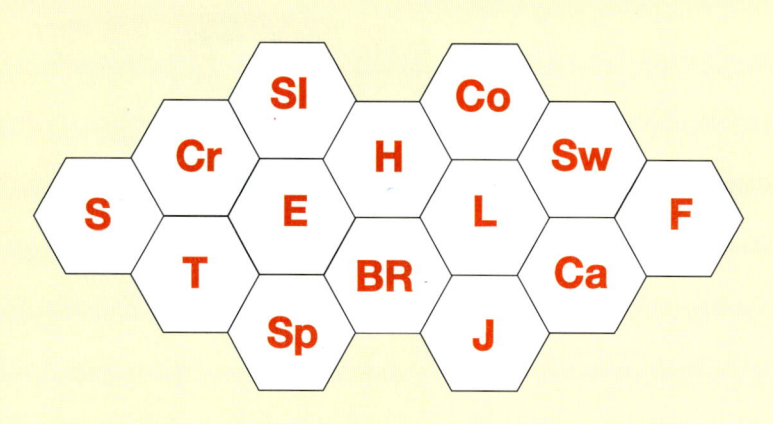

```
     Sl      Co
  Cr    H      Sw
S    E     L      F
  T    BR    Ca
     Sp   J
```

T	The rainforest is	BuR	Tree support
Sl	The slowest animal in the whole world!	Co	Only living things are allowed in here!
E	Its members can be living or non-living.	J	Very fast – in more ways than one!
Sp	All of one kind.	Sw	You could get bogged down in one of these.
H	This could be a chain store shop!	Ca	Overhead protection?

• TOP TIPS •

Remember that communities and ecosystems are *not* the same! Communities are made up of the living things in an area – but ecosystems include other things, that aren't alive, such as air and rocks.

Food web

Finish this food web by adding arrows to show which predators eat which prey. (Use the information on the diagram opposite to help you). The arrowhead should point to the prey, not the predator in each case. The example shows you how to do this.

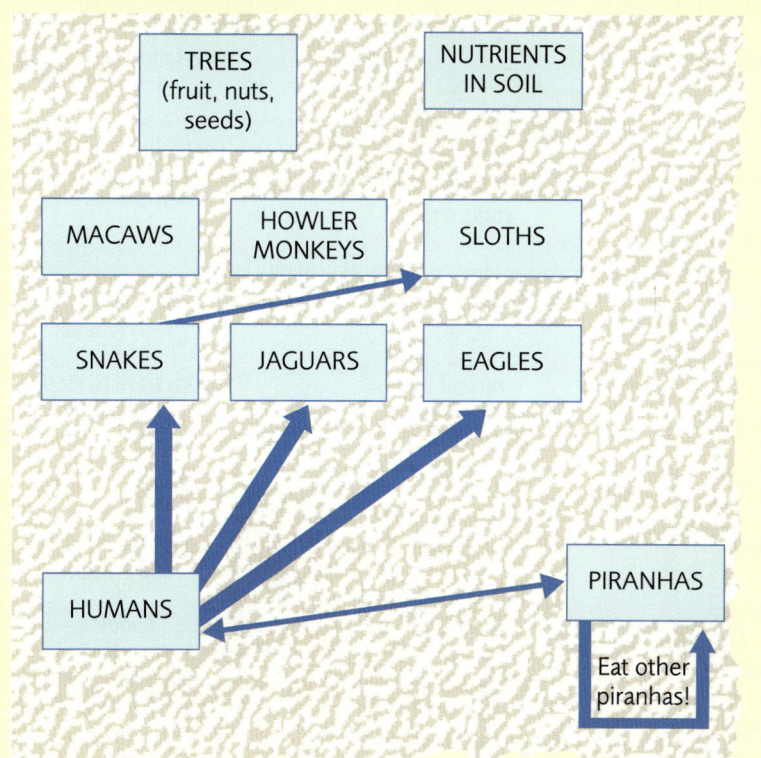

```
    TREES                NUTRIENTS
  (fruit, nuts,           IN SOIL
    seeds)

  MACAWS    HOWLER      SLOTHS
            MONKEYS

  SNAKES    JAGUARS     EAGLES


                        PIRANHAS
  HUMANS                Eat other
                        piranhas!
```

KEY FACTS

↑ Animals like Musk Oxen, which live in very cold biomes like the coniferous forests, have double layered coats to keep them warm.

→ Animals like snakes and lizards that live in hot deserts are often cold blooded, as this helps them to cope with the very high temperatures.

↓ Elephants living in the savanna grasslands have learned how to survive its seasonal droughts by pushing over baobab trees and breaking them open to get at the water stored in the tree trunks.

It's a worm's world!

'Hi! My name's Yani and I'm a fat juicy earthworm living in the soil under the tropical rainforest. Life's pretty OK down here – although we do get waterlogged after heavy rain. There's lots of food for me and my team of <u>decomposers</u>. We eat and <u>recycle</u> the leaves and animal droppings from the forest above us. Doing this provides the trees with the <u>nutrients</u> they need to grow well. We may be small and rather unattractive but we provide a very important service. Without us, the whole forest ecosystem would grind to a halt.'

All ecosystems work like the one Yani has talked about. Their different components work together and depend upon each other.

If just one component changes, the whole ecosystem can break down – and some plants and animals may even become <u>extinct</u>. The diagrams below show what can happen when deforestation (cutting down trees) takes place.

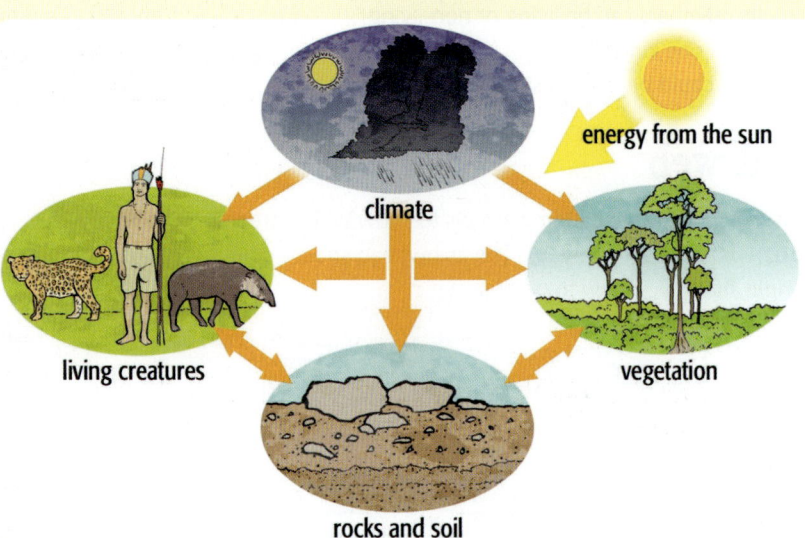

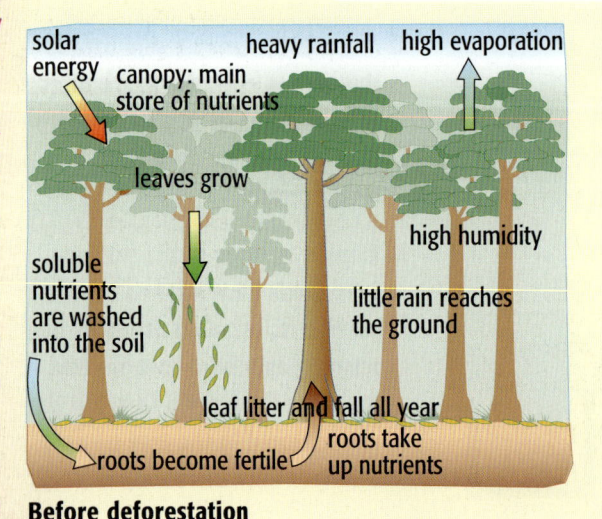

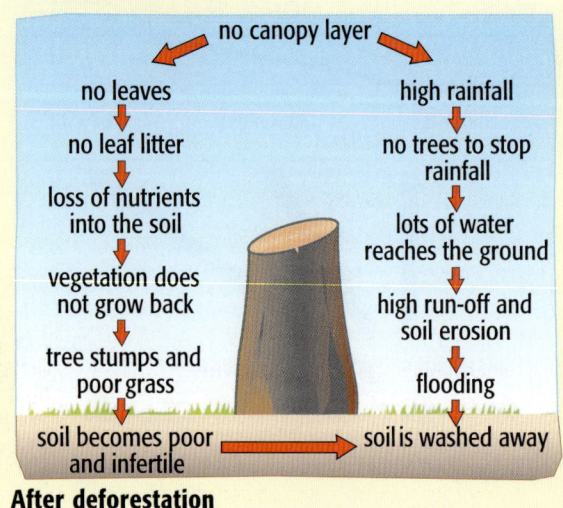

climate

energy from the sun

living creatures

vegetation

rocks and soil

Before deforestation

- solar energy
- canopy: main store of nutrients
- heavy rainfall
- high evaporation
- leaves grow
- high humidity
- soluble nutrients are washed into the soil
- little rain reaches the ground
- leaf litter and fall all year
- roots become fertile
- roots take up nutrients

After deforestation

- no canopy layer
- no leaves
- high rainfall
- no leaf litter
- no trees to stop rainfall
- loss of nutrients into the soil
- lots of water reaches the ground
- vegetation does not grow back
- high run-off and soil erosion
- tree stumps and poor grass
- flooding
- soil becomes poor and infertile
- soil is washed away

Rainforest riddle

There is one word hidden in each circle to the right. Use all of the letters in each circle to discover the hidden words.

True or false?

Write a 'T' in the box to show which of these statements you think is true; use an 'F' for any that are false.

☐ Worms are the only decomposers in tropical rainforest soils.

☐ Decomposers are important because they provide trees with nutrients.

☐ Few insects can survive in tropical rainforest soils.

☐ The Sun is the source of energy for all ecosystems.

☐ Both plants and animals can affect the soil in an ecosystem.

☐ Deforestation is what happens when trees are chopped down.

Write down three differences between the before and after deforestation pictures on page 64.

....

....

....

KEY FACTS

⬆ **Soil takes thousands of years to develop. It is a mixture of weathered rock particles and organic material (dead animals and plants). Without soil, plants cannot grow.**

➡ **Tropical rainforests are rich, tall and dense, but the soil they grow in is often only one metre deep and very infertile.**

⬇ **Thousands of different species of insects and fungi live in every cubic metre of tropical rainforest soil.**

⬆ **Tropical forests are constantly being cleared for logging timber, mining valuable minerals, growing crops, grazing farm animals and building new roads and towns.**

⬆ **Trees take carbon dioxide from the air and put oxygen into it. Animals do the opposite, which is why trees and animals need each other in order to survive.**

• TOP TIPS •

Trees protect the soil beneath them against heavy rain. Rain can soak through the soil, taking its nutrients much deeper under the surface – a process called <u>leaching</u>. It can also erode the topsoil, by washing it away.

Test your knowledge 8

1 Name the three continents that have large areas of tropical rainforest.

....

(3 marks)

2 a) Complete this climate graph using the temperature and rainfall figures in the table below it.

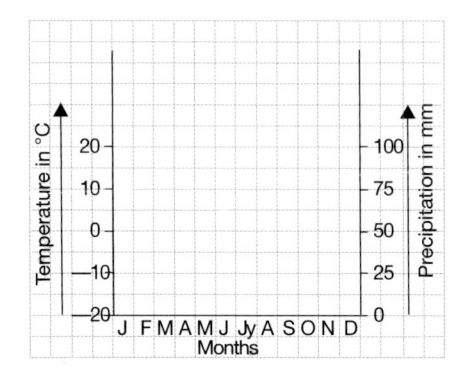

	J	F	M	A	M	J	Jy	A	S	O	N	D
Temperature in °C	−12	−10	−4	0	5	10	13	12	8	0	−5	−9
Rainfall in mm	25	22	23	25	34	54	75	56	48	40	38	38

(4 marks)

3 a) List four ways in which tropical rainforest trees have adapted to their natural environment.

....

....

....

....

b) Now list four ways in which acacia trees have adapted to difficult climate conditions.

....

....

....

....

(8 marks)

4   Finish this rainforest cross-section diagram by writing suitable labels in its boxes.

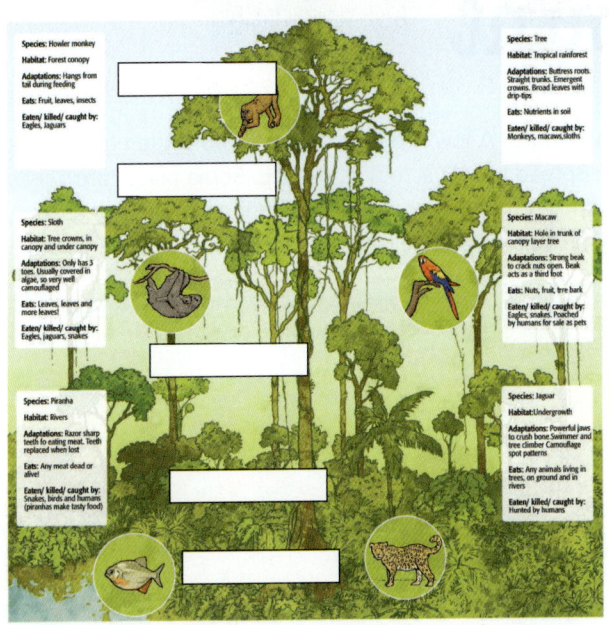

(4 marks)

5   Use these words to finish this sentence:

communities   ecosystems   interact   species

Different .... of animals and other kinds of living things ....
with each other to form ...., which also interact with the non-living parts of
their environment to form ....

(4 marks)

6   a) Finish this diagram of an ecosystem by labelling all four of its circles.

b) What is the source of energy for all ecosystems?

....

(5 marks)

7   Write short definitions to give the meanings of these important words.

Decomposer   ....

Leaching   ....

Nutrient   ....

Recycle   ....

(4 marks)
(Total marks 32)

People count

Most people live in villages, towns and cities. A few live in small, scattered settlements like farmhouses and tiny villages. The world's population isn't spread evenly across its surface. Some places are very densely populated (they have a lot of people per km²), while other places have sparse population densities (they have far fewer people per km²). The labels around the map give some of the reasons for this uneven distribution.

For the last 150 years, the size of the world's population has grown very quickly. This is shown in the graph below and has been so fast that geographers say that there has been a population explosion. The graph also shows the expected population growth to 2050.

Every minute, 247 babies are born around the world, 107 people die and the total population increases by 140. This may not seem a lot, but the fact file below shows you the effects of this natural increase (the difference between birth rates and death rates) on the world's population.

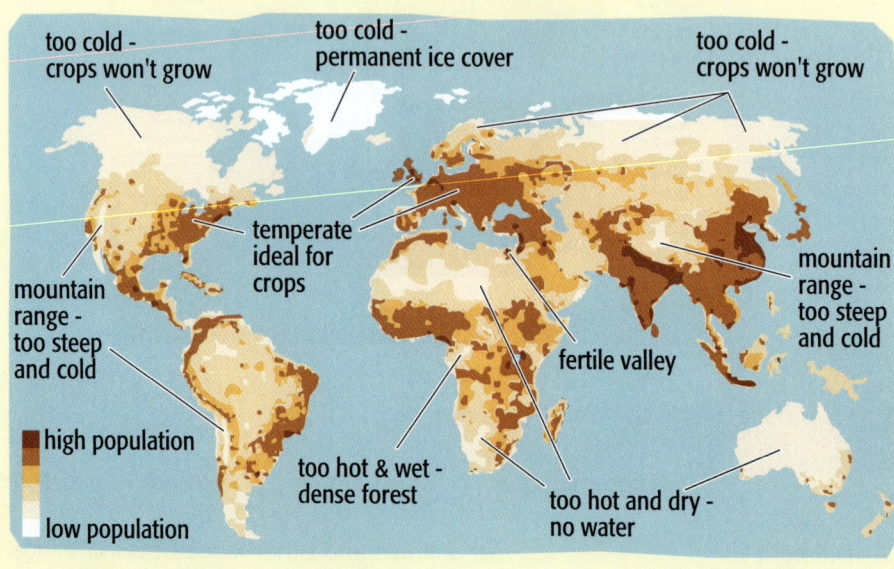

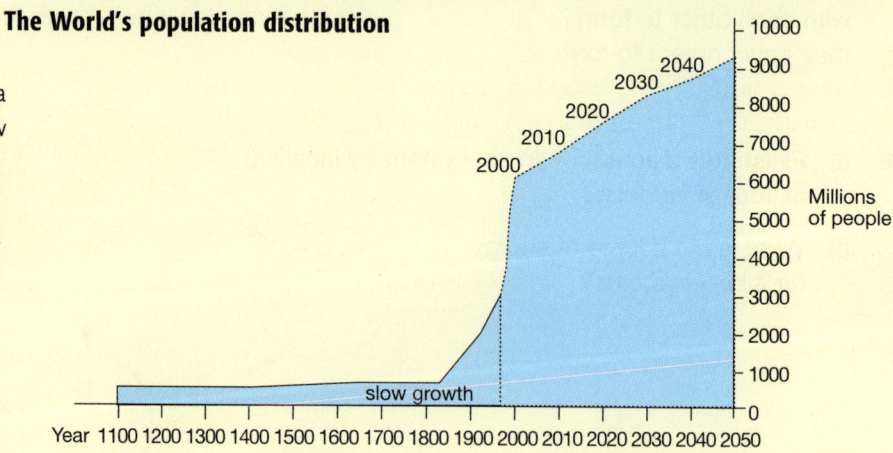

Map labels: too cold - crops won't grow; too cold - permanent ice cover; too cold - crops won't grow; temperate ideal for crops; mountain range - too steep and cold; mountain range - too steep and cold; fertile valley; too hot & wet - dense forest; too hot and dry - no water

The World's population distribution

The world's population explosion

Fact file

Time	Births	Deaths	Natural increase
Hour	14 842	6 408	8 434
Day	356 201	153 781	202 419
Month	10 834 440	4 677 520	6 156 919
Year	130 013 274	56 130 242	73 883 032

There are many reasons for this rapid population growth, but the most important one is a fall in the death rate (the number of deaths per 1000 people per year). Better health care and diets mean that many more people are living longer.

Population puzzle

The 10 most highly populated countries	Population in July 2005	The 10 most densely populated countries	Number of people per km²
China	1,306 million	Bangladesh	1,002
India	1,080 million	Taiwan	636
USA	296 million	Palestine	605
Indonesia	242 million	Korea	492
Brazil	186 million	Puerto Rico	430
Pakistan	162 million	Netherlands	395
Bangladesh	144 million	Lebanon	368
Russia	143 million	Belgium	340
Nigeria	129 million	Japan	337
Japan	127 million	India	329

1. Can you suggest reasons why China and the USA are not densely populated even though so many people live there?
   ....
   ....

2. Why are countries like Taiwan, Palestine and Puerto Rica densely populated?
   ....
   ....

3. Use the information in the table below to complete the timeline at the bottom of the page; projected population figures for the 21st century are shown in red. Two labels for 1805 and 1927 have been written in to help you.

1805	1927	1960	1974	1987	1999	2013	2028	2054
1 bn	2 bn	3 bn	4 bn	5 bn	6 bn	7 bn	8 bn	9 bn

4. How many years did it take for the world's population to increase:

   a) from 1 billion to 2 billion? ....

   b) from 5 billion to 6 billion? ....

   c) Is the *rate* of population growth expected to increase or decrease in the first half of the 21st century?
   ....

KEY FACTS

↑ Population density is calculated by dividing the area of the land in km² by the size of the population.

→ Some places that are very difficult to live in *can* be densely populated. This happens where valuable minerals such as oil, gold and diamonds have been found. The deserts of Western Australia and Alaska are good examples of this happening.

↓ In the past, women usually had many babies and birth rates were high. However, natural increase stayed low because most babies died before their fourth birthday.

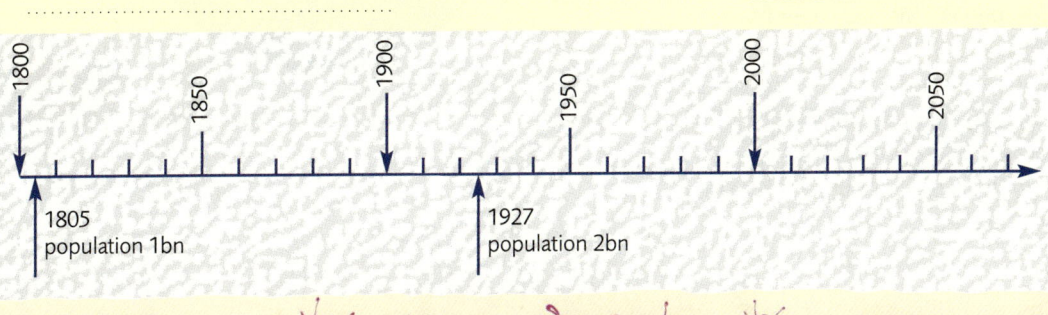

1800 | 1850 | 1900 | 1950 | 2000 | 2050

1805 population 1bn

1927 population 2bn

Well dry!

Do you leave the tap running while you clean your teeth? Most people do, and that wastes a huge amount of safe, clean water every year. We live in a country that usually has enough water for us to drink, shower, water the lawn, wash the car and do lots of other things as often as we wish. Because of this, it's very easy to forget that one in six of the world's poorest people struggle to get enough water just to drink and cook with. 40% of the world's population face serious water shortages. Such shortages are likely to become a much more common and widespread problem – creating a global water crisis that is bound to affect those of us who live in the UK. Water is a far more vital resource than food. We can survive for only a few days without water, but supplying

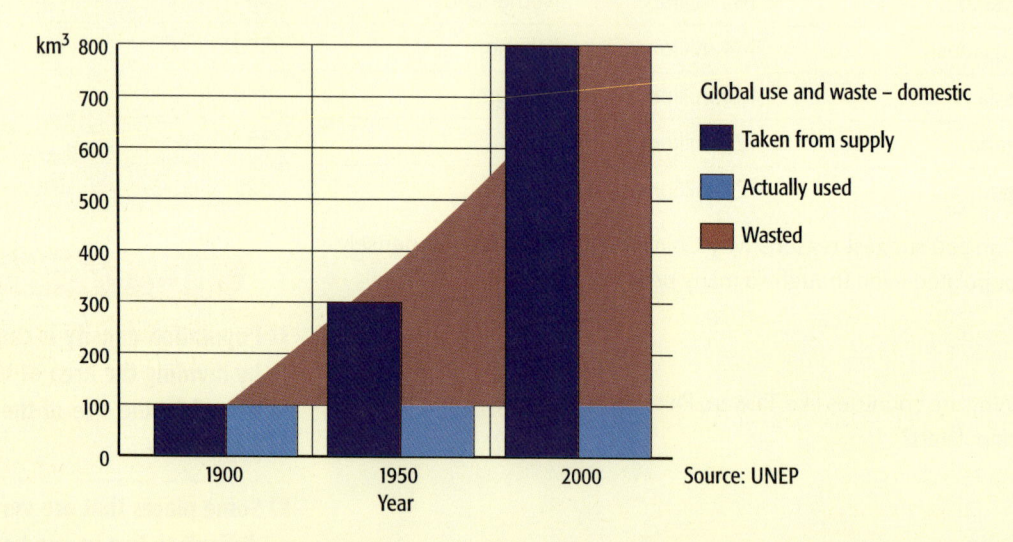

Global use and waste – domestic
- Taken from supply
- Actually used
- Wasted

Source: UNEP

the world's increasing population with it becomes more difficult every year. The pie chart shows that, although most of Earth's surface is covered by water, very little of it is freshwater (not salty water). It also shows that most freshwater is either frozen or stored below the surface as groundwater – often so deeply that we cannot extract it for use.

The world's population and water use per person are both increasing, but the amount of water available for people to use is not. Matching water supply to demand is difficult, for lots of reasons. One of these reasons is that the world's population is not spread evenly across the Earth's surface and neither is the rainfall. Areas such as California have many people but have very little rain, while others (like the Amazon Basin) have a lot of rain, but few people. Moving water from areas of high rainfall to areas of great need may seem to be the answer but doing this is very difficult and hugely expensive. Sometimes, it would also need countries to cooperate with each other but, unfortunately, this rarely happens.

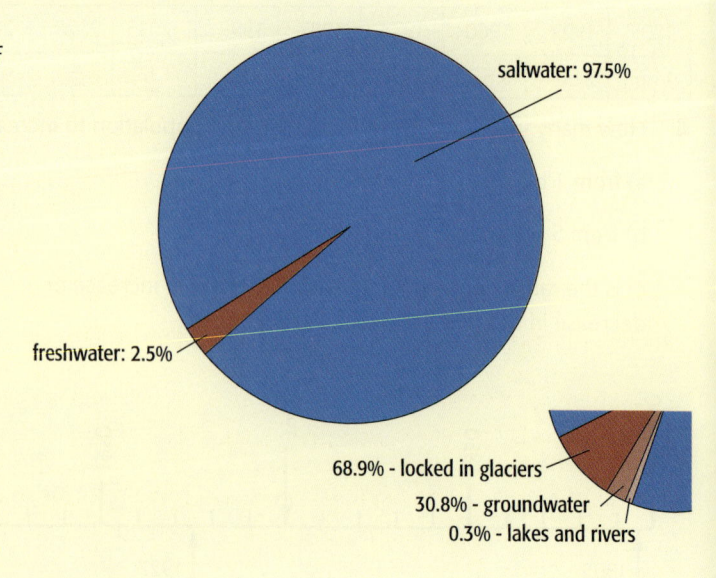

- saltwater: 97.5%
- freshwater: 2.5%
- 68.9% - locked in glaciers
- 30.8% - groundwater
- 0.3% - lakes and rivers

Water use wordsearch

Complete this wordsearch by looking for water uses in MEDCs. There are 18 different activities hidden in the grid.

W	A	S	H	I	N	G	C	A	R	Y	T	G	L	O	M	Y	O	Y	T	K	U
A	W	Q	U	R	I	J	L	E	R	H	H	E	O	L	N	R	I	H	G	J	Y
T	E	U	J	E	U	H	E	R	E	F	E	S	N	I	A	T	N	U	O	F	T
E	R	I	N	D	Y	G	A	T	W	R	R	E	U	H	K	S	U	H	D	G	D
R	D	E	M	H	T	F	N	Y	K	E	E	D	Y	G	J	U	Y	G	F	F	O
I	S	T	R	I	R	D	I	S	J	W	Y	E	T	F	H	D	T	F	G	D	G
N	A	M	E	P	E	S	N	D	H	S	D	N	A	H	G	N	I	H	S	A	W
G	W	O	S	A	W	E	G	F	H	D	O	D	R	T	G	I	K	D	M	A	A
L	A	U	N	D	R	Y	C	G	G	E	L	F	E	E	F	T	J	S	R	S	S
A	T	M	A	D	I	S	H	W	A	S	H	E	R	E	D	R	H	D	A	F	H
W	E	E	S	L	R	W	P	E	E	E	L	S	W	T	D	E	G	G	F	G	E
N	R	N	D	I	O	I	E	A	D	D	O	A	S	G	S	F	L	H	E	H	F
S	I	T	F	N	I	M	N	H	S	F	T	W	D	N	N	M	H	J	L	J	G
R	N	O	G	G	U	M	F	K	D	T	H	E	F	I	A	I	G	K	B	K	H
H	G	R	E	P	Y	I	E	M	I	T	O	R	G	N	S	H	H	E	A	K	H
G	F	S	R	O	T	N	R	L	R	N	R	R	H	A	D	E	E	T	R	L	J
F	L	A	U	O	R	G	S	K	G	E	G	E	A	E	F	N	D	A	A	L	E
E	O	S	F	L	U	S	H	I	N	G	T	O	I	L	E	T	F	S	A	B	R
A	W	B	F	M	M	D	E	G	N	I	K	O	O	C	F	Y	B	D	S	K	S
S	E	R	V	N	N	T	H	H	G	B	R	T	K	E	M	A	D	F	D	J	A
O	R	G	I	V	B	Y	E	G	B	V	E	R	J	W	N	I	R	G	F	H	S
L	S	R	A	C	G	N	I	H	S	A	W	E	H	D	B	Y	S	M	G	E	D

• TOP TIPS •

In some places like India, rainfall is seasonal and is followed by several months of drought every year. Rain can also be very unreliable, for example in countries such as Mali. Other countries, like Egypt, receive almost no rain at all and rely completely on water from the rivers flowing through them.

Where's the water?

Fill in the blanks in this paragraph, using the words and years listed below it. You will need to use some of the words twice, and leave some others out completely.

2012	America	Asia	Australasia	Brazil	Canada	England	equatorial	Europe	hot deserts
India	MEDCs	NICs	North America	Russia	scarcity	USA	water	2025	

By the year ...., every continent will have times of water .... Africa and .... will be most badly affected, but ...., ... and .... will also have problems. Only South .... will be relatively free of them. Many of the areas affected are already ...., but much of central .... isn't and this will be badly affected as well. The problems will not only affect the poorer LEDCs but also .... and the rich .... The colder areas of the world like .... and .... are not expected to have many shortages and, because they also get a lot of rain, the .... areas can also expect to be all right. South eastern .... can expect to have water .... However, Scotland can look forward to having sufficient ....

KEY FACTS

▸ Water is a <u>renewable</u> (reusable) <u>resource</u>; shortages occur because we keep using more and more of it.

▸ In countries that have seasonal droughts, more water evaporates from reservoirs, lakes and rivers than is used by the whole human population every year.

▸ People in MEDCs use *ten times* more water than people in LEDCs, partly because they use more of it for non-essentials like watering the lawn. Modern industry and agriculture also use vast amounts of water.

▸ Many LEDCs can't afford to build the large reservoirs needed to store enough water in order to meet demand and survive droughts.

Dying for a drink?

It is now believed that over 50% of the world's population will not have enough water by 2025. Hundreds of ecosystems around the world will have been destroyed because there will be little water left for plants and animals. If our natural <u>habitats</u> are seriously damaged, plants, animals and people who live within them will be put in danger. While advanced technologies may be able to find alternatives for resources like oil and gas as they run out, water is irreplaceable. We have to drink and we have to be able to grow crops for food.

Although the ideas in this picture may seem extreme for the UK at present, similar restrictions have previously been used during periods of drought and are likely to become even more common in the near future. In water-rich countries like ours, we take our supply for granted and often waste water – by cleaning our cars with a hosepipe instead of a bucket and sponge and overwatering lawns by leaving sprinkler systems running longer than is necessary.

In water-deprived areas, people have to use water in more <u>sustainable</u> ways. They value it more highly, because it is much scarcer. The sustainable use of any natural resource, such as water, means not wasting it, reusing it as much as possible and using it in ways that doesn't harm the environment. People like ourselves who live in MEDCs aren't good at doing this yet, but we *will* have to become good at it. If future generations are going to have sufficient water and food, every country will have to develop effective water management and <u>conservation</u> programmes.

The Government can:	You can:
• Build a reservoir	• Put brick in toilet cistern
• Maintain mains water pipes	• Use the shower instead of the bath
• Pipe water to areas of water scarcity	• Don't leave the tap running
• Build wells	• Reuse washing-up water for watering the garden
• Encourage traditional irrigation	• Wash car with bucket of water

Water conservation strategies

Water-saving word snake

1 List each of the water-saving suggestions hidden in this word snake.

....
....
....

Word snake contents: TURNOFFTHETAPSTOPUSINGTHEDISHWASHERFILLTHEWASHINGMACHINEFULLYMULCHTHEGARDENFITARAINBUTTTAKEASHOWERDONTBATHUSEABUCKETANDSPONGETOCLEANTHECARUSERAINWATERTOWATERTHEPLANTSORREUSETHEDISHWASHERWATER!

2 Choose the three water saving suggestions from the snake that you think would be most effective, then write a reason why you've picked each one.

Choice 1 .... because ....

Choice 2 .... because ....

Choice 3 .... because ....

KEY FACTS

- In South Africa, all water supplies are now metered. Every person in the home is allowed to have 50 litres per day free – and all other water has to be paid for. Doing this has dramatically cut the country's water consumption.

- Most modern irrigation methods waste lots of water because they provide the plants with more than they need and can actually waterlog the soil, drowning the plants instead of helping them to grow.

- Some car wash companies use recycled water. This is a more sustainable way to clean cars because it means that pure water is saved for drinking and cooking.

- Fitting a water tub to collect rainwater from the roof is a very sustainable way of watering the garden. This water would otherwise be lost into the drains and sewage systems without being used.

• TOP TIPS •

Rich, hot desert countries such as Kuwait have so little water that they use desalination plants. These convert sea water into freshwater by removing its salt, but this is a very expensive way of providing water. Another way might be to tow huge icebergs to water scarce areas. South east England is already thinking of importing water from Norway by using huge floating tanks.

Test your knowledge 9

1 Pair up these key words with their correct meanings:

> birth rate   death rate   densely populated   natural increase
> population explosion   sparsely populated

.... is how we describe places where few people live near to each other.

.... is how we describe places where many people live near to each other.

.... is the difference between birth rates and death rates.

.... is the number of births in a year per 1000 people.

.... is the number of deaths in a year per 1000 people.

.... is what we call the very rapid increase in the world's population over the last 150 years.

(6 marks)

2 Use ticks to complete this table. You may use more than one tick on each line.

Country name	One of the world's largest populations	One of the world's most densely population countries
China		
India		
USA		
Indonesia		
Brazil		
Pakistan		

(10 marks)

4 a) List any four activities using water *that are essential for healthy living*.

....

....

74

b) Now list another four activities that involve using water, but that *aren't* essential.

   ....
   ....

   (8 marks)

5 Draw three bars on this graph to show the percentage figure for each label under the graph.

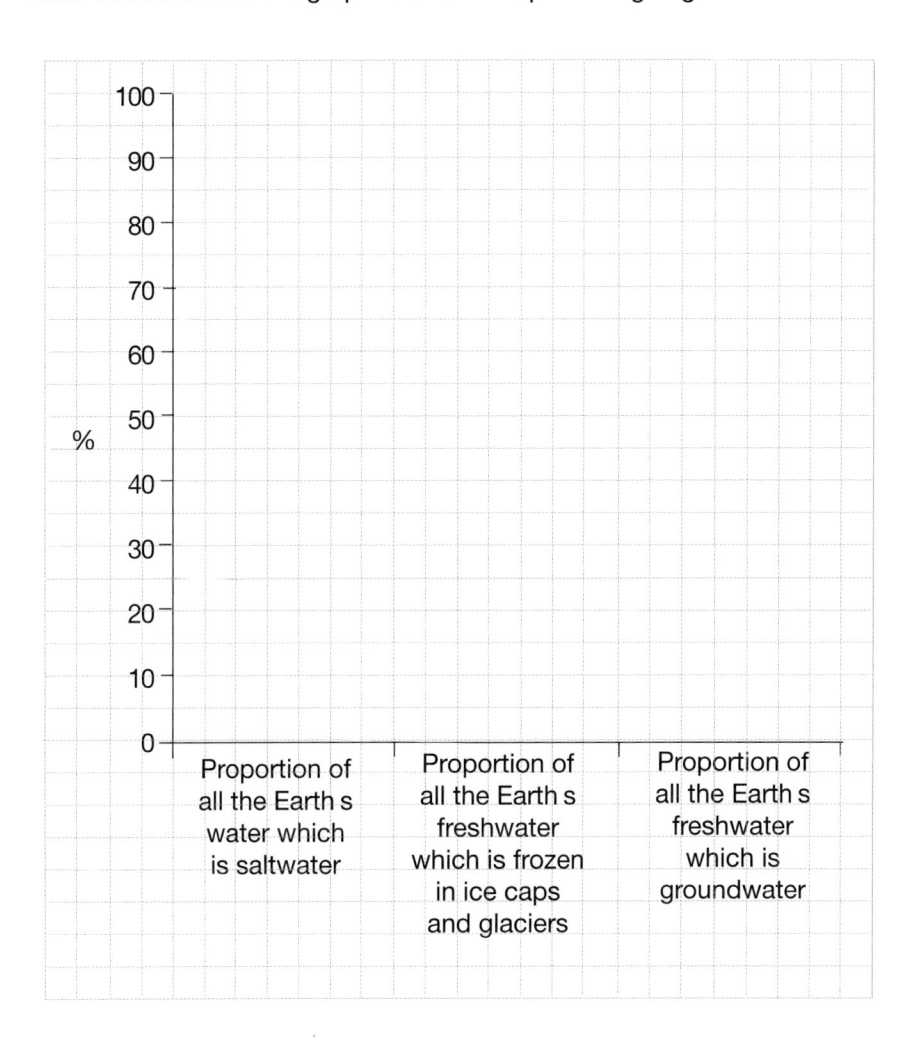

%

100
90
80
70
60
50
40
30
20
10
0

| Proportion of all the Earth's water which is saltwater | Proportion of all the Earth's freshwater which is frozen in ice caps and glaciers | Proportion of all the Earth's freshwater which is groundwater |

(5 marks)
(Total marks 29)

Glossary

Altitude Height above sea level.
Backwash Water moving down a beach after a wave has broken.
Bay Eroded section of coast between two headlands.
Beach Area of sand or pebbles along a coastline.
Beach replenishment Replacement of sand that has been transported from a beach by longshore drift.
Biome Large community of plants and animals that has adapted to live in a particular climate zone.
Birth rate Number of live births per thousand people per year.
Blow-hole Crack in the top of a cliff, formed when part of a cave roof collapses.
Central business district (CBD) Urban area at the heart of a town or city, which is dominated by shops, offices and public buildings.
Chain store Shop that is part of a nationwide group such as Boots, Next and Top Shop.
Cliff High and extremely steep rock face.
Climate Average weather over a long period of time.
Community Group of plants and animals that share the same habitat.
Condensation Change from water vapour into liquid water due to cooling.
Conflict Disagreement between groups of people carrying out different activities or holding widely differing opinions.
Conservation Using natural resources in ways that cut wastage and extend their availability for future generations.
Continentality Effect of distance from the sea on weather and climate.
Convection rainfall Rain that falls when air is heated by the Earth's surface and rises; it then cools and clouds form.
Corner shop Small, isolated shop providing a housing area with low-order goods.
Death rate Number of deaths per thousand people per year.
Decomposer Any consumer of dead plants and animals.
Deforestation Deliberate clearing of forested areas by cutting or burning.
Densely populated Many people living in an area of land.
Deposition Laying down of material such as sand, which has been eroded and moved by wind, water or ice.
Depression Area of low atmospheric pressure.

Developmental indicator A measure of wealth or standards of living in a country.
Economic activities Primary, secondary or service jobs (see separate definitions).
Ecosystem A community of plants and animals *and* their natural environment.
Erosion Wearing away of the land surface by wind, water or ice.
Ethnic group Group of people that is different from the majority of the people living in a country because of their ancestry, culture or customs.
Evaporation Change of liquid water into a gas known as water vapour.
Extinct Plant or animal species that no longer exists because all of its members have died.
Favela Brazilian 'shanty town'. A rapidly growing, illegal settlement of homes often built from scrap materials; usually found on the outskirts of a town or city.
Front Boundary between warm and cold air masses within a depression.
Frontal rainfall Rain that falls when warm, moist air rises over colder, drier air.
Gabion Steel-mesh crate, filled with boulders, used to protect coasts against wave erosion.
Geo Very narrow, steep-sided inlet eroded into a cliff face.
Gross domestic product (GDP) Measure of a country's wealth averaged out per person.
Groyne Breakwater down a beach built to slow the movement of material due to longshore drift.
Habitat Specific environment in which communities of plants and animals live; their 'home'.
Headland Area of high land jutting out into the sea.
High-order goods Items that are expensive and bought less often, e.g. televisions, fridges and cars.
Hydrological (water) cycle Recycling of water from oceans to the atmosphere then to land and back again.
Hypermarket Very large supermarket selling a much wider range of household goods; often has other service providers (e.g. hairdresser, optician and travel agent) on site.
Immigrant Person who has moved to a new area or country to live permanently.
Interact Share a habitat with other species in a way that affects how they live.
Latitude Distance north or south of the Equator, measured in degrees (°).

Leaching Rain soaks through the soil taking nutrients out of each of plant roots.
Less Economically Developed Country (LEDC) Poor country with a low level of economic development.
Longshore drift Movement of beach material along a coast.
Low-order goods Items that are cheap and bought regularly, e.g. milk, bread and newspapers.
Mental image Idea about a place based upon information that has been seen, read or heard. It may, or may not, be accurate!
More Economically Developed Country (MEDC) Wealthy country with a high level of economic development.
Multinational company (MNC) Large business with offices or factories in many countries around the world.
National park Large area of great natural beauty and wildlife that is protected by law from new developments.
Natural increase Increase in population due to birth rate exceeding death rate.
Nature reserve Small area of land and/or water in which wildlife and plant communities are protected.
Newly industrialised country (NIC) LEDC which has experienced rapid growth in its secondary (manufacturing) industries and so is becoming more wealthy.
Nutrient Food needed by plants and animals in order to live.
Pedestrianised Area in which roads are closed off to motor traffic.
Platform Gently sloping wave-cut rock surface found at the foot of a coastal cliff.
Population explosion Very rapid increase in population size.
Precipitation Water (in any form) that falls from clouds.
Prevailing wind Most frequently occurring wind direction over a particular area.
Primary industry Activity that provides natural raw materials for human use.
Process Any way in which a change can take place.
Recycle Reuse a resource in a way that protects the environment and/or slows the use of its valuable raw materials.
Reef Area of rock remaining when a stump has been eroded down to sea level; often covered at high tide.
Regional shopping centre Huge retail site with over 100 shopping units of all sizes. Has extensive, free car parking and is often next to a motorway junction.
Relief Shape and height of the land surface.
Relief (orographic) rainfall Rain that falls when moist air is forced to rise over high land.
Renewable resource Raw material needed to sustain life that is continuously replaced or naturally recycled.

Retail park Modern shopping development away from the CBD; its shop units are usually very large and share an extensive car park. Normally located next to a main road.
Retail trade The selling of goods.
Rock armour Large boulders placed at base of cliff to absorb wave energy and so reduce erosion.
Secondary industry Manufacturing industry turning raw materials into finished goods
Service industry (also known as 'tertiary industry') Industry that provides services to individuals (e.g. hairdressing) and other industries (e.g. banking).
Settlement Any place in which people live permanently.
Shopping hierarchy Arrangement of shopping facilities in order of size and importance.
Shopping parade Small group of shops, providing a range of low-order services such as post office, newsagent, greengrocer and fish and chip shop.
Sparse population densities Few people living in an area of land.
Species Group of plants or animals that look alike and are different from all other groups of plants and animals.
Spit Curved ridge of deposited sand or pebbles resulting from longshore drift.
Supermarket Large, single storey, self-service store selling food and other household items, with its own large car park.
Sustainable Way of using natural resources to meet present demands while ensuring that the needs of future generations will be met.
Swash Water moving up a beach from a breaking wave.
Synoptic chart Weather map recording conditions in the atmosphere – such as air pressure, temperature, cloud cover, wind speed and wind direction.
Temperature range Difference between the maximum and minimum temperature across any period of time.
Transnational corporation (TNC) Alternative term for MNC.
Transportation Movement of eroded material.
Tropical rainforest Vegetation that has adapted to live in equatorial climate areas.
Water vapour Invisible, gaseous form of water within the atmosphere.
Wave-cut notch V-shaped hollow at the base of cliff caused by wave action at high tide.
Wave-cut platform Gently sloping ledge of rock left when a cliff face has been completely eroded.
Weather State of the atmosphere at a particular time of day or night.
Weathering Breaking down of rocks by biological, chemical or physical action.

Answers

Odd one out p5
1 cliff   2 because it's a feature not a weathering or erosion process.

Word jumble p5
abrasion, physical action, attrition, hydraulic action, chemical reactions, biological action.

Erosion crossword p7
Across: 1 Wave cut platform, 5 Blow hole, 6 Beach, 9 Stump, 14 Headland, 15 Geo, 16 Cave, 17 Stack
Down: 2 Collapses, 3 Reef, 4 Bays, 8 Sand, 10 Tide, 13 Crack

Name the features p9
Mainland, sheltered lagoon, new saltmarsh, spit made of sand or pebbles, sea and longshore drift.

Coastal protection p13

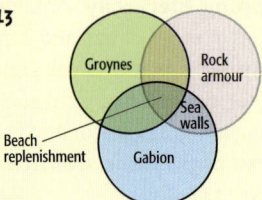

(Venn diagram: Groynes, Rock armour, Sea walls, Beach replenishment, Gabion)

Seaside wordsearch p15

Beach pairs p15
Examples of answers could include:

First activity	Second activity	Reason for conflict
Exercising dogs	Children playing on the beach	Dog faeces are a health hazard.
Swimming	Water skiing	Swimmers can be injured or killed by boats or skiers

Word jigsaw p17
CARAVANPARK
FIRINGRANGE
SHIPWRECKAGE
OILPOLLUTION
FACTORYSPILL
TRAFFICJAMS
SANDDIGGING
WINDTURBINES
OILDRILLING

Shopping list p21
corner shop: butter, newspapers, sugar, tins of corned beef; town centre: furniture, towels, toys, school uniform

Days gone by p21
wireless, scrubbing board, gramophone, mangle

Where do you shop? p23
- Retail park with warehouse stores
- High street shops
- Newsagents, corner shops and petrol station shops

Internet – good or bad? p25
A, A, A, D, A, A, D, D, D

Follow the order p25
Log on to your chosen company's website; place your order on the webpage; Internet server sends your order to the company's warehouse; chosen items taken off the shelves and packed; goods sent by post; parcel arrives at your home.

Rain jumble p29
estel = sleet, nari = rain, ilah = hail, nows = snow

Fill the gap p31
1 North Sea   2 Bay of Biscay   3 The Pyrenees   4 The Alps
5 Baltic Sea   6 The English Channel   7 Arctic Circle
8 Mediterranean Sea   9 Iceland   10 The Black Sea

Rainfall quiz p31
1 A front forms where warm air meets cold air.   2 As air rises, it cools and condensation occurs.   3 As air sinks, it warms and evaporation occurs.   4 Convectional rainfall is formed when air is forced upwards by strong heating.   5 Convectional rainfall is most common in Europe in hot summer weather.   6 If air is very hot, it rises quickly and cumulonimbus storm clouds form.   7 Much less relief rain falls on the leeward (or rain shadow) side of hills.
8 Relief rain is heavier on the windward side of mountains.
9 Warm air is light and rises; cold air is heavier and sinks.

Weather wordsearch p33

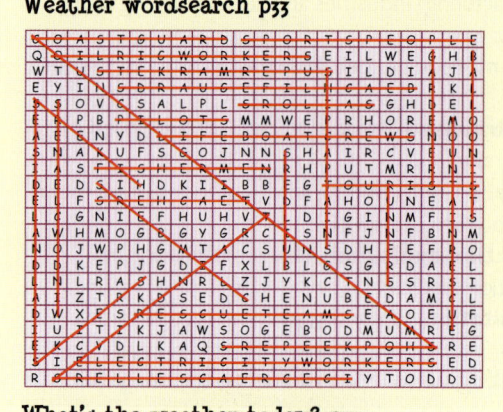

What's the weather today? p33
Examples of possible answers include:
Rescue workers need to know what the weather is like so that they can equip themselves appropriately – and so that they can be ready on stand-by for poor weather conditions. *Shop owners/ice cream sellers* need to know what customer numbers are likely to be (people's shopping habits vary with the weather) and what goods to stock, e.g. de-icer if frost and snow are forecast.
Pilots/ships' captains because bad weather (especially fog) affects their ability to navigate, land (or get into port); their planes/boats might be at risk, e.g. in storms at sea or thunderstorms in the air. Flight/sailing times and routes may change – they may have to take the decision to divert once the journey has started.

Climate jigsaw p37
OCEANICCURRENTS
LATITUDE
CONTINENTALITY
COASTALLOCATION
TOTALRAINFALL
PREVAILINGWINDS
ALTITUDE
SOUTHERLYASPECT

Climate contrasts p39
A – north, B – east, C – west, D – south

Climate crossword p41
Across: 1 Insulate the roof, 3 White washed walls, 8 Heated garage, 9 Olives, 10 Wheat, 12 Snow ploughs, 15 Central, 16 Skiing, 17 Heating
Down: 2 Snow mobile, 4 Triple glazing, 5 Steep roofs, 6 Keep animals, 7 Barley, 10 Wrap up well, 11 Light clothing, 13 Saunas, 14 Grow vines

Images of Brazil p45
a) A shows….., B shows …., C shows ……, D shows ….., E shows;
b) There is no correct answer for this question – it is whatever you believe; c) Various answers possible. Depends on students' interpretation.

Brazilian brainteaser p47
1 approximately 4250 km north south, approximately 4600 km west east   2 area = 8.5 million km²,   3 34 times larger   4 most – Amazonia or north or Equatorial region, least – north east, highest – Amazonia or north or Equatorial region, lowest – South.

Brazilian life p49
1 Words are: plantations, cotton, sugar cane, coffee

North east Brazil	South/south east Brazil
Cotton	Coffee
Plantations	Cotton
Sugar cane	Plantations

2 A: north east, B south/south east, C north east

Industry quiz p53
1 primary industries: fishing, mining, farming; secondary industries: shipbuilding, oil refining, steelmaking; service industries: policing, selling, teaching
2 arable farming, life expectancy, unemployment, literacy, infant mortality rate, poverty   3 poorer   4 poorer

Brazilian crossword p55
Across: 1 Germany, 2 Italy, 3 Iron ore, 4 Gold, 5 West Africa 6 Japan, 7 Bahia, 8 Sugar cane, 9 Coffee, 10 Brazilia, 11 Portugal, 12 Sao Paulo
Down: 13 Rio de Janeiro

Import/export quiz p57
1

S	C	I	E	N	T	I	F	I	C	E	Q	U	I	P	M	E	N	T
W	O	O	D	P	U	L	P		M	E	D	I	C	I	N	E	S	
T	U	R	B	O	~	J	E	T	S		F	O	O	T	W	E	A	R
P	L	Y	W	O	O	D		F	E	R	T	I	L	I	Z	E	R	
C	A	R	~	E	N	G	I	N	E	S		W	H	I	S	K	Y	
I	N	S	E	C	T	I	C	I	D	E	S			G	O	L	D	
P	O	U	L	T	R	Y		S	O	Y	A		M	O	T	O	R	S
M	E	A	T	e	s	p	e	c	i	a	l	l	y	B	E	E	F	

2

Brazil's exports to the UK	Brazil's imports from the UK
wood pulp	scientific equipment
footwear	medicines
plywood	turbo-jets
gold	fertilisers
poultry	car engines
soya	whisky
meat – especially beef	insecticides
motors	

Tree adaptation p61
Acacia: deciduous leaves drop in the dry season; long tap roots can reach water deep underground; roots spread outwards to get water from a wide area; thick bark protects tree from fire damage in hot weather; small, waxy leaves reduce loss of water.

Fir: conical shape/flexible branches allow snow to slide off; seeds are protected against cold within cones; roots are shallow because lower soil layers are permanently frozen; thick bark gives protection against cold weather; thin, wax covered leaves called 'needles' protect the tree from frost bite and reduce water loss in summer.

Gold run p63
Cr Crown; T Trunks; Sl Sloth; E Ecosystem; Sp Species; H Habitat; BuR Buttress Roots; Co Community; L Lianas; J Jaguar; Sw Swamp; Ca Canopy

Food web p63
Tropical, sloth, ecosystem, species, habitat, buttress roots, community, jaguar, swamp, canopy.

Rainforest riddle p65
SOIL, DEFORESTATION, INSECTS, RECYCLE, DECOMPOSER, NUTRIENTS, ECOSYSTEM

True or false? p65
F, T, F, T, T, T

Population puzzle p69
1 The area of the country is very large.
2 The area of the country is very small.
3 a) 1bn–2bn: 123 years b) 5bn–6bn: 13 years c) It will decrease.

Water use wordsearch p71

Water-saving word snake p73
2 Your answers could include:
Turn off the tap because otherwise more water is wasted than you will actually use! Stop using a dishwasher because it uses *much* more water than it takes to wash up in a bowl. Fill the washing machine fully because the same amount of water is used to wash a full load as is used to wash one or two small items. Mulch the garden because this stops evaporation from the soil and means the plants need to be watered far less often.

Test your knowledge 1
1 erosion, weathering 2 erosion processes: abrasion, attrition, hydraulic action; weathering processes: biological action, chemical reactions, physical action 3 Correct order is: weathering, erosion transportation, deposition 4 from top to bottom: crack in cliff face, cave, arch, stack, stump, reef 5 (see page 6) 6 (see page 6) 7 a spit 8 deposition 9 laterals (or curved hooks) 10 It is a sheltered area with deposition of material. This raises the area above sea level and allows salt-marsh plants to grow.

Test your knowledge 2
1 groynes, rock armour, gabions and sea walls 2 No answers required 3 a) answers from: holiday park, hotels, caravan sites, camping sites b) car parks, public toilets, public telephones, museum, golf course, public houses, country park, National Trust Property, cycle network, national trail/long distance path c) farming, church ministers, builders, house repairs and maintenance, electricians and plumbers, pub landlord/lady, warden d) nature reserve; National Trust property.

Test your knowledge 3
1 Retail 2 Low-order goods: bread, comics and magazines, milk, potatoes, sweets; higher-order goods: black and white TV,

furniture, shoes, washing machine, watches. 3 chain stores, garage forecourts 4 hypermarket 5 Examples include: go to the cinema/watch a film, go bowling, eat a meal, go on rides, have a coffee or cola, have things like watches/shoes repaired, go window-shopping, go to opticians for eye-test, have hair cut/styled. 6a) i Braehead ii Metro Centre iii Trafford Centre iv Merry Hill v Meadowhall vi Cribb's Causeway vii Lakeside viii Bluewater b) London, c) Braehead, d) no 7 Examples include: debit and credit cards, store cards, fridges, freezers, the Internet, bar coding of goods.

Test your knowledge 4

1. rain, sleet, hail, snow
2. Hydrological cycle   3 fall (or drop)
4. Condensation: change from water vapour to liquid water (droplets). Evaporation: change from liquid water to water vapour (gas). Precipitation: moisture falling to earth/ground from clouds e.g. rain.
5. 1) Surface run-off, 2) channel flow, 3) water table, 4) ground water store.
6. Your answer should be something like:
   Heat from the sun evaporates sea water. Moist air is blown towards the land. When this moist air meets higher land, it has to rise. As it rises, it cools. Cool air cannot hold as much water vapour (or moisture). Therefore, condensation occurs. This forms clouds. If the clouds rise higher, they cool more and so rain occurs. After the air has passed over the high land, it starts to sink and it is warmed. The clouds evaporate and the rain stops over the rain shadow area.
7. Convectional rainfall

   sun — 5 cloud grows
   4 condensation — cumulus cloud
   3 air cools
   sun's heat — 2 warm air rises — 6 rain falls
   1 ground surface heated

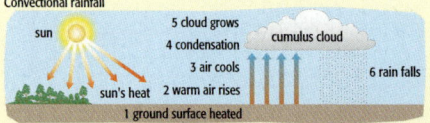

8. Computers allow forecasters to handle huge amounts of information from many weather-recording stations very quickly. They also turn this information into maps. Additionally, they can compare the present atmospheric conditions with past events stored in their memories and use this to suggest possible weather conditions over the next five days.
9. Satellites allow weather forecasters to 'see' the weather that is heading in our direction.
10. Answers could include: pilots, ships' captains, fishermen and yachtswomen, shops, rescue services, gritting teams, tourists, sports/leisure people, electricity companies, tourists, hoteliers/landladies.

Test your knowledge 5

1. T, F, T, T, F, T
2. A is climate 4; B is climate 2; C is climate 1; D is climate 3.
3. Almost no, hotter, colder, colder, less
4. a) warm, dry b) summer c) south
5. prevailing winds, temperature range, aspect, altitude, latitude
6. weather, weather, weather, climate, weather

Test your knowledge 6

1. Portuguese, Brasilia, football, Reàl, carnivals, oil, drought
2. ocean 1: South Atlantic; Tropic line 2: Tropic of Capricorn; range of mountains 3: Guinea Highlands; river 4: River Amazon; river 5: River Paraná; city 6: Belem; city 7: Brasilia; city 8: Rio de Janeiro
3. D is not true; it should say: The Brazilian flag has four colours: blue, green, yellow and white. E is not true; it should say: The north east of Brazil is much poorer than the south/south east. F is not true; it should say: Most of Brazil lies in the Southern Hemisphere. H is not true; it should say: Brazil has 27 states, but only five main geographical regions.
4. Climate graph A: north east region. Reasons: high temperatures all year, seasonal drought; Climate graph B: south/south eastern region. Reasons: warm all year (or hot in summer, warm in winter), rain falls all year – but not as much as in the north. (Alternatively, not as hot nor as wet as the northern, equatorial, region); Climate graph C tropical rainforest/Amazonia/North. Reasons: very high temperature, no variation in this temperature all year, no seasons, very high rainfall all year.
5. Problems include: overcrowding, poorly built, small houses, no proper roads, no shops.

Test your knowledge 7

1. T, T, T, F, T, T
2. Literacy rate; average GDP/person; infant mortality rate; population living in poverty; population with internet access.
3.

Century	Events happening in this century
Sixteenth	Discovery by Portuguese sailors
Sixteenth	First West African slaves arrive
Seventeenth	Gold discovered in Minas Gerais State
Eighteenth	Coffee first grown in Brazil
Eighteenth	Rio de Janeiro becomes the capital city
Nineteenth	Brazil becomes independent of Portugal
Nineteenth	Coffee becomes the main export crop
Nineteenth	Immigration of Germans and Italians begins
Twentieth	Brasilia becomes the new capital city
Twentieth	Brazilian 'economic miracle'

4 *poor:* less economically developed country (LEDC), newly industrialised country (NIC), *rich:* more economically developed country (MEDC)   5 Possibilities include: Portuguese and other Europeans brought diseases like measles that wiped out huge numbers of native Indian peoples; the Europeans turned them into slaves and made them work so hard that many died; forest clearances have robbed them of their homes and way of living so more have died.   6 1500, around 1850, 1960   7 Primary industries: coal miner, forestry worker; secondary industries: oil refinery worker, shipbuilder; service industries: teacher; airline pilot 8 Plywood, footwear and gold are imported by the UK; medicines, fertiliser, insecticide and whisky are imported by Brazil. 9 HQs are in MEDCs; factories are in LEDCs.   10 transnational corporations.

Test your knowledge 8

1. South America, Africa, (South east) Asia
2. a) [climate graph showing Temperature in °C and Precipitation in mm across months J F M A M J Jy A S O N D]
3. a) tall, layering, little undergrowth, emergents, evergreen forest – each tree loses individual leaves as they die, buttress roots
   b) deciduous leaves drop in the dry season, long tap roots can reach water deep underground, small waxy leaves reduce loss of water, thick bark protects tree from fire damage when hot.
4. Emergents, main canopy, under canopy, shurb layer, ground layer
5. species, interact, communities, ecosystems
6. a) A – climate; B – living animals; C – vegetation/plants; D – rock and soil.
   b) the sun
7. Decomposer – any consumer of dead plants and animals. Leaching – washing away of minerals and nutrients from soil by rainwater. Nutrient – food needed by plants and animals in order to live. Recycle – reuse a resource in a way that protects the environment and/or slows the use of its valuable raw materials.

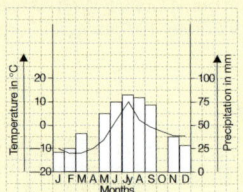

Test your knowledge 9

1. sparsely populated, densely populated, natural increase, birth rate, death rate, population explosion
2. China ✓, India ✓✓, USA ✓, Indonesia ✓, Brazil ✓, Pakistan ✓
3. a) Select from: drink, prepare food, flush toilets, wash hands, clean cooking and food utensils, clean food preparation surfaces, wash food. b) select from: water flowers/lawns, clean windows, wash the car, scrub patio/paths, wash the dog.
4. 97.5%, 68.9%, 30.8%